ISBN 978-1-838236
A Salt Swan Publishing

# IN SEARCH OF THE SWAN

# Contents

## CHAPTER ONE

### *THE BEGINNING*

I remember as a young child of no more than eight years of age being suddenly awoken one night, getting up from my bed and finding the windows of our prefabricated home wide open. The television was also switched on and its sound on full volume. We could hear the sound of metal chains rattling in the hallway. I remember also seeing the fridge door flung wide open. The front and back doors also wide open. All this after the family had retired to bed, locking all of the doors, turning the television off etc, etc. This was not an isolated incident.
For two weeks these strange goings on would continue. They also appeared to be increasing in intensity. I still remember my dad telling his brother Kenny who visited us one evening about the strange occurrences. The goings on had scared the wits end out of the whole family, but what had caused the strange happenings? Who would believe such nonsense? Certainly not my uncle Kenny who was in fits of laughter as we told him the story.
He suggested to my dad (in a rather sarcastic way) that if what he was being told was all true, then a large mirror that sat above the mantel piece would fall down. A large grin ascended upon his face as he said it. Within seconds of his comments, the large mirror crashed to the floor shattering into a thousand pieces leaving the whole family stunned. Kenny laughed no more. The screams descended down the street. It was such a shock! God knows what the next door neighbours must have thought!

The remarkable thing was once that mirror had fallen, the goings on were no more. We never did find out what it was or what had caused it. It was unexplainable and as time moved on it became a distant memory. Until many years later when I would become as close to the world of the unexplained as you could possibly get. So close in fact I would become the dead poet's pen.

I was brought up like most children through an educational system that left little room for free thinking. My time at school was pretty much by and large wasted. I can't remember ever enjoying school. In fact I looked forward to the bell at home time more than the lessons. Hours of endless meandering of the mind consuming little of the then educative diet on offer. My capacity to sit and endure the day at school never quite reached expectations. I left school covered in shame after being expelled aged 15 and with a blank canvas for a mind, which was in time to become my greatest asset. A blank canvas that gave me a freedom, a freedom to explore life from a somewhat different perspective than would have been possible had I achieved through an educational means.

The road I have travelled since those early years has not been easy, far from it, but through the mind I have experienced a totally new reality.

Existence for me from my schooling years was one big dose of misspent youth. A rather cavalier attitude to life. A couldn't be bothered sort of attitude. A 'begin and end with me kind of attitude'.

I was born in Plaistow in London's rough, tough East End. The land of what I would call the 'duckers and divers' where someone would knock on your door and say would you like to buy a television? How about some carpets? It was the norm! I also remember a friend telling me about someone he knew who had knocked on his door and said to him "do you want to buy this radio cassette?" He took one look at it and said "that is my radio cassette!" It goes to show you can't trust anyone! The East End is full of characters, some of them not so nice, but the East End is a place I enjoyed being brought up in. Coming from a happy family background, a good many friends and an appetite for life in the raw or so I thought, instead I found that the reality was that I saw myself aimlessly going through life's dilemmas in my own uncouth way. Taking from life as much as I could and one would have to admit giving very little in return. I look back now with some horror but that's the way it was. I did have some fun, some great laughs but my downfall was a love affair with gambling. Blighted by a near addiction since I was 21 and one which brought me to my knees on numerous occasions and one which ultimately brought not only misery to me, but misery to others around me, especially those I loved. Why do it if it has that affect on others? Good question!

The gambler dreams of the big win, the one to free them, but from what exactly? I couldn't honestly tell you. The dream of just winning that 'big one' tormented me. It meant that each bet I'd have would secure me at least another chance of that dream being realised. It would buy me at least another ticket to change my life and elevate me from the rat race and the struggle, perhaps that's the answer… the rat race and the struggle? Well, that was the plan! The thrill of that elusive big win kept me intoxicated. The unfulfilled dream, the easy life.

The place the bet it comes up, then I'm all right jack kind of dream! Alas, year upon year the same repetitive patterns. The same non-committal me. The same old lack of responsibility. A life rather empty, a shallow and meaningless existence.
A life going absolutely nowhere, when suddenly WOW! The big win. Well part of it!
Stephen Hendry perhaps the greatest snooker player these shores have ever produced turned the final of the Benson and Hedges Masters Tournament on its head by beating Mike Hallett in an incredible final nine frames to eight. This after trailing by seven frames to one and then by eight frames to two. Mike Hallett caught stage fright and his attempts to get over the winning line floundered. It was as if his cue tip had been replaced by a rather large house brick. His nightmare became my dream, as the tears of Hallett's despair turned to my ecstasy. To say I couldn't believe my eyes was an understatement. My thousand pound bet at the bookmakers Corals had become almost twenty thousand pounds. At last the bookmakers turn to pay, from almost nothing to a rather fat wallet. I turned up at the bookies with a grin as wide as the ocean and requested a cash payout much to the despair of the shop manager, it certainly was a luvly jubbly moment. Twenty thousand may not be that life changing, but boy it did me the world of good. Within days of collecting my money I bought cash down a £15,000 325i BMW convertible, red in colour with black leather interior. I went off clubbing the same night and met someone. Bang, head over heels. Knowing nothing at all about her, yet falling in love all in one night. There she stood long flowing curly black hair, with a face that only an angel could compare. A dress so tight that looked as if it has been painted on.

A vision that made my beating heart still and this dream was destined to sit beside me in the wheels. Fantastico! How life had turned in the space of a few days. Three months later, it was talk of the Wedding. Expensive ring and all. A pre-booked holiday took my beloved away for two weeks and it couldn't have come at a worst time. Feeling bored I felt it a good time to rekindle my love affair with the gambling. Wrong move! Unfortunately the betting shop was still my bank and the funds were dwindling faster than sand through spread fingers. It was simply awful. A disaster of the 'everything will go if you're not careful variety!' And so it proved. The BMW just had to go and with it so went the wedding, the girl and life sure had hit a bad spot. Love had been an illusion. A magic trick. Now you see, it now you don't! Bring out the loaded gun! Desperation then realisation!

In my head turmoil. Left with just over five thousand pounds, the BMW's replacement (a second hand Ford Sierra) whose only comparison to the BMW was that the window wipers worked, I set out to win her back. Just imagine it. Holy sh*t! What a state to be in. BMW to a Ford Sierra? Boy, that's tough to bear! Love struck, blinkered and besotted and just like all sane and sensible individuals would do in this position yep, I bought a house! Five thousand down and a mortgage big enough to tempt the large bottle of Paracetamol from the top shelf into my tea. The desperation of course was trying in vain to win her back and the realisation was that it was now all over. So too were the days of the thousand quid in the back pocket. Now it was back to the poor man with no girl, no love and just a bloody great mortgage. Praying to God for some

salvation and feeling sorry for myself. Sitting on the floor of an almost empty three bedroom house in a pretty part of Essex, now my reality and the stupidity of my previous existence dawning.
A drowning man who swam like a rock.
Life was now no longer fun and I no longer secure in my little world of self-delusion. Sitting on the floor of a sparse home with very few items was indeed a real eye opener. I did all I could to make it home. Another win would make it alright wouldn't it? Of course it would and when I did get any decent money, it seemed that everything I gambled on fell, pulled up, went lame, dropped dead or was just about fit for a milk round. At times a monkey (£500 quid) rode on those b*stards. Imagine £500 quid falling at the first, bloody painful believe me! I began to feel the world was against me. I could feel myself spiralling into oblivion. My health began to go down. Depression set in, dark moods swinging my personality from someone who liked a laugh to someone devoid of a sense of fun and purpose.
I remember one particular day looking at my wristwatch. The time said eight twenty am, I then turned to look up at a rather cheap wall clock I had bought and saw it said ten past three! I flew into such a rage the clock flew from the wall with one hefty whack, alas never to tell time again. It's never easy confronting yourself and the days were drifting by and six months after my move I was as near rock bottom emotionally as I could possibly get. Thankfully no drugs or alcohol, the gambling was bad enough! Friends were becoming distant memories. I had just about lost interest in all and sundry. No one knew or could know my despair.
I went to bed early one evening with hands cupped and prayed for some more divine intervention.

At least a winner or two! Please dear God if you're listening and if I am not being too greedy can you deliver me another big one? Just a few grand will do! I tried to prompt God for some angelic wings for my jockeys, but the following day watched again as one by one they floundered as if intoxicated. One particular horse dumped the irate jockey off as the flag was raised, my ticket was torn in so many pieces it became unrecognisable.
I arrived home that night irritable as per usual and retired early to bed not knowing my life was about to change forever. Not financially, but in a way I could never have dreamed possible. The following morning on awaking, I felt surprisingly good within myself. That morning anyway I was like a spring lamb rather than a bear with a sore head, no money but I felt really good for a change. I felt like the cloud of despair that had hung over me for weeks had suddenly evaporated into thin air. For the first time in months I actually heard the birds sing that morning. Boy I felt good! Even though I hadn't a pot to piss in and no milk in the fridge for a cup of tea, and I just couldn't have cared less. It was an unexplainable feeling. For me being pot less and clueless about where my life was going was hardly the right recipe for floating on a cloud and yet, this elated feeling had the desired effect of making me want to write. Oh for God's sake! Me write? Write what for heaven's sake? A song? A love letter? A poem? A biography? Don't be silly! I didn't write anything unless it was betting slips! In haste I took a pen and pad from the draw and sat to write. To my amazement I began to write. Without thinking of any subject matter and most surprisingly of all, not only was I writing but my pen began to move rapidly, with words tumbling

out of the pen and onto the virgin white paper, like a snake spitting venom. Good gracious I thought! The paper began to fill like a well at rain time. The words kept flowing like an endless stream. My heart started to beat at a rapid rate. After filling both sides of the paper I sat aghast. I was absolutely stunned! In just over the time it took a kettle to boil I had filled two sides of A4 sized paper with writing and yet not a single thought had entered my head. Just where had these words come from if I had no thoughts? It was a most bizarre happening. On the paper there was no punctuation, no grammar and yet the wording was totally fluent. Not a single thought had entered my head and yet before me were pages of writing with over 260 words on them. I must explain at this point that at no time did I feel that someone or something was controlling my hand when I wrote. I felt a tingle spread throughout my body as the realisation came that the writing in front of me was not that of my own thought process but from some unexplainable source outside of my understanding. It appeared to me having begun reading what had been written, that this was a conversation taking place and that the recipient of these words was me! Where on earth were these thoughts/words coming from if not from me? I was completely baffled. Had I lost the plot completely? Had the stresses and strains of watching the nags beating hasty retreat finally delivered unto me a mortal blow of the sanity kind? Looking at the words on the paper I could see that the writing had a personality far different from that of my own. Some of the words written down I couldn't even read let alone have written them. I needed a dictionary to understand their meaning. It was totally bizarre.

I must admit I found the whole experience quite frightening at first, but when I calmed down a little and was able to digest it, I realised I was being told things by someone or something from somewhere outside of my logical train of thought or understanding. I found it all fascinating, amazing even but difficult to comprehend. Writing was not my forte. The wording seemed to indicate that my life was pre-destined. This prompted me to telephone an old friend and try to explain it in a 'simple' yet understandable way. He in his wisdom declared that I was "completely f****** mad". "Come over and see for yourself!" I told him. "Give me twenty minutes and I will be over" he replied (laughing as he put the phone down).
He arrived at mid-day with a grin on his face and said "this had better be good. I have just driven ten miles for this!" As he walked through the door for some unexplainable reason I grabbed his left shoulder with my right hand and squeezed it gently in a cupping motion. He appeared a little startled by my actions (which you would do wouldn't you?) then he stepped back. He suddenly started to rotate the left arm in a clockwise direction. "I can't believe it" he said. "I couldn't do that before I came here! I busted my left arm in karate years back. I have had restricted movement in it ever since. What on earth did you just do?" I didn't have a clue, all I knew was that for some unexplainable reason I had grabbed his shoulder. Dean seemed convinced it had somehow magically healed his problem. At this point I was wondering if I and now Dean had lost the plot. Still trying to recover from that shocker he then got another. He sat down and read the piece of paper I had written. "Who wrote this?" He said.

“Me!” “Na” “I told you it was weird” “Weird” he replied.... “It’s f......crazy”. He looked rather shell-shocked. He then looked again at the wording. “It doesn't sound like you at all?” “Do you think you could write again with me here?” “Write again?” “I don't know?” “I will give it a go”.
I picked up the pen and placed it on the paper and began to write just as before. Once again no thoughts had entered my head as the page rapidly filled with words. I then turned over the paper and continued writing. This time over 200 plus words were written without pause. “I can't believe the speed you wrote that” said Dean. “It’s just incredible!” “I know what you mean” I replied. "What does it say then”? “Right, let's have a look. Here we go, it says,” as I began to read it his face dropped visibly. He spluttered on his tea (leaving stains all over the carpet and nearly choking in the process) as the words from the paper gave up their contents. Personal details began to unfold, things regarding his life that I had never known. The writing then talked about his wife Donna’s Doctor’s appointment which had taken place the previous day. This brought from him an accusation that I had been having an affair with his wife? He said “Do you know my wife?” “No, I replied, but thanks for the tip.” (An affair with his wife? Ding Dong!) Now that would have been nice). He telephoned her straight away and she confirmed she hadn’t seen me for over five years! My friend having had the chance to dissect the paper had realised, that what had been written content wise was NOT by me. “You wrote it for sure, I can see that! But it’s just not you is it? If I had not seen it with my own eyes I would never have believed it” he added. It seemed to me I was merely an instrument to convey a

message but from whom and where? "How do you explain it Dean?" "Don't ask me," he said. An hour or so later Dean had left still trying to comprehend the experience. From the information I had been given future events predicted for my friend came true. This meant that not only did the writing require explanation of how it had magically come about in the first place, but how on earth was the future predicted? The information given was so accurate. So much so in fact that it near frightened him to death and I haven't seen him since well maybe once or twice. I don't think he has ever recovered! After the first two attempts I began to write as often as possible and to my amazement it worked every time. Please bear in mind that my hand was not moving automatically at any point. If I stopped the writing would stop. If I began to write again the information would return. The only difference between what I was doing and what any normal person would accept as writing, were that the thoughts were not my own. How could I possibly doubt it after my experience with Dean?
I was totally perplexed as to its source, but it was there before me in black and white. It appeared to give me accurate information about things I never knew beforehand. It was by any stretch of the imagination a complete mystery. It was simply astonishing! Yet it happened and it was very real. The whole concept of what I understood to be reality seemed distant to me. I was certain this was not my own mind but that it was from some other extraneous source, of which I had no understanding. I was writing the thoughts of someone or something else that I could not see, feel, hear or touch but I knew existed somewhere out there beyond my rational mind.

# CHAPTER TWO

## *THE DEAD POETS PEN*

Ladbrokes or should that be Lad-broke? Anyhow Ladbrokes is known as the magic sign in gambling terms and that sounds about right! It was magic how they took so much money from me. Gambling can be if not dealt with correctly so destructive, it almost destroyed me. Life is about learning but boy I wish I had learnt early, that gambling isn't the best road to go down. To go along with the gambling I found a new struggle in my life the writing as it began a conflict of mind. I had become two people. One person which the gambling made selfish, obnoxious, angry and pushing the button which said self-destruct, the other a gentle soul who was beginning a road of enlightenment. My very own two loves of comfort and despair. I found a great comfort in the communicative writing and of course the despair was in the gambling. It was during a moment of despair whilst writing that I was given the name of my one of my 'ghost writers'. "My name is John," he said and that he would be my guide to help me along my journey of life. It all seemed so surreal. After all it is not every day that you write and are a secretary basically for someone who you cannot see, hear, smell or touch, but this was exactly what it was. The writings were from somewhere outside of my world and now I had a name for some of this unknown, unseen source of writing, its author John. No second name just John.

It seems far-fetched I know but how could I or anyone doubt what I was saying? After all I had the writings in front of me. All in black and white and giving me such accurate information I could not possibly have known. If it was me and my own mind, then how do you explain the great speed of thought that enabled me to write so fast? Without ever pausing to stop? Or think of what to write next? Or that I had information not previously known to me? Or for that matter the fact that future events predicted would come true? I asked others to try to replicate what I was doing but they simply couldn't. So whatever it was that I was doing wasn't normal, otherwise anyone could have done it. But they couldn't! I kept looking for rational answers but there simply weren't any!

What was John? Who was John? That was the question? He became so familiar to me in the coming weeks through the communicative writings that I came to accept him as part of me. I would want to try to talk to John even when the faller at the last fence had taken my last ten quid and with it my friendly side. I'd go home from the bookies and kick the imaginary cat. The gambling at times was a monster inside me. To the outside world I might have portrayed myself as a strong man but my fundamental weakness was my vulnerability for greed. It's a greed that entices many gamblers! Or was mine just desperation to change my life? I would have to say it's both! Greed in as far as the more you win the more you want. But hang on a minute, you rarely win! You're just deluding yourself in a world of total delusion. I must confess I even wondered if John would give me some inspired tips but he never did. And I must confess I did ask. I guess John wasn't a punter? He was however an inspiration. My pen was his pen. My paper was his paper. My hand was his hand. John was a real part of me. John would often talk in metaphorical terms when I wrote. I had difficulty comprehending some of his riddles at times, but it at least made my mind work overtime with trying to decipher the meaning of it all. I enjoyed the puns etc, but they were frustrating because only the passage of time would reveal their hidden meaning. Every hour spent reading John's words were indeed an hour of total fulfilment. I had to believe that John was real and not some wild piece of imagination simply because it had been proven to me. To me it was a total reality. My dear pen friend from some far off distant land, who judging by the messages flowing through my pen could see all and was aware of all that was going on. He could see the past, the present and the future. He could apparently see all before him. Was this a communication with the dead? I for one wasn't prepared to make such claims, but I wasn't going to rule anything out at this point either. It did remind me of the incident as a young child with the doors and windows opening, television on and the mirror falling etc, because I thought to myself that if that was some kind ghostly activity and they could physically make things happen, then why couldn't they communicate through writing, using me as an instrument? I was frankly open to any suggestion in order to bring some reason and some sense to it all. What could possibly give reason to my experience? No one could explain it, and neither could I. It was an enigma which was to get even more unbelievable as time progressed.

I remember waking one morning (some three months or so since my first experience) and before my eyes were properly opened picking up the pen for another writing session. It was then that I began to hear the words for the very first time. I didn't hear words in the sense of it being audible to my ears, but as a voice in mind. What I could only describe as a thought voice (just like the imagination). John told me that I would embark on the most extraordinary journey and experience incredible things along life's road. He told me he was my teacher and I his pupil and that there would also be others who would communicate through me. Though I learned very little whilst at school John and co would give me an education beyond anything I could ever have gleaned from textbooks. He and the others would teach from their school of thought. I was so excited by the prospect of being re-educated. Just then more mundane things popped into mind like the daily chores. After getting ready I put on my jacket, left the house and locked the front door behind me. I remember thinking how lucky I was to have this ability and was very excited by its potential to change my life. Just perhaps I would be able to change the lives of others too?

I took a short bus ride into Basildon town centre (not too far from where I lived at the time) and came across a shop window which caught my eye. I felt very drawn towards the shop; I must admit it was a rather strange feeling. The shop sold trinkets of all descriptions. I walked in and went up to the counter where for some unknown reason began to tell the story of my strange happening to the shop assistant. Strangely it felt right to discuss it with her. To my astonishment she listened intently not finding my conversation strange at all. On the contrary I found she appeared to be engrossed with it. After I had finished she told me it was fascinating and told me about a friend of hers who she felt I should meet. On giving me a business card she said "Give this lady a call. She would love to speak to you." How strange it was to come across this shop and a person able to accept what I was saying! I just couldn't understand why I told the shop assistant in the first place or indeed why she would be the remotest bit interested in the story. Nevertheless, I took the card said "thanks" and left. Looking at the card in my hand I saw a name on it, it read Shileen. That's an unusual name I thought to myself. I then proceeded to look further down the card. It read Psychic and Tarot reader. It gave me goose bumps. Psychic and tarot reader sounds interesting. Putting the card in my trouser pocket I was unable to believe I had told anyone about the writings and about John, especially someone I had never met or spoken to before. No one knew of this John, not even my own family. It was such a difficult subject to approach. Who would listen? Who would believe me? Well, the shop assistant for one! However; I was quick to learn that my ability would not be readily accepted by many, nor would I be readily accepted as someone who was sane and telling the truth. My experience of people's reaction to the story led me to keep it all secret. Many people who I had told the story no doubt had laughed behind my back. It seemed people just didn't understand. I didn't blame them for if someone had told me the same story some months before I got the ability I am sure I would have thought it a little farfetched. Well you would wouldn't you? This was going to be terrible to live with if I couldn't talk or share it with others. Even my family thought I had flipped. And if those who love you think that, then you know it's going to be one hell of a tough burden to shoulder. I wanted to tell the world, but at this point in my life it just wasn't to be. So what was I to make of the card given to me that day in the shop? Psychic & Tarot reader? Was I risking my own sanity pursuing these roads? Where would it all lead? Perhaps I was already in the throes of madness? If not mad, then just on its edge! I was unable to assimilate the irrationality of it all. Talking with an unseen friend via pen and paper! Perhaps I was going mad? Perhaps it was all an act of self delusion? But I was certain I wasn't going mad and a self delusion it certainly wasn't. I was beginning to build an immunity against any kind of conventional thought, but the thing was would anyone listen? I was too strong in my conviction to worry about that. I knew it was true in my heart and until someone could prove otherwise that's the way it would stay. I knew John was for real, although I had no logical answer to his sudden intrusion in my life. What I did know was that life was never going to be the same and my understanding of reality was never going to be either.

The weeks had flown by since John's first words and I felt very comfortable communicating with him. I was now spending every conceivable moment I could with a pen in my hand. Each day I wrote I just never knew what might come through, as the pen embraced the paper. I found myself being in a position totally isolated from the world outside. Normal conversation was no longer of interest to me, even the television set no longer appealed. I felt

myself changing, my life was changing. This happening had totally consumed me. I was becoming withdrawn, pretty much conversation-less in terms of friends and family. Setting aside my gambling and all the conceivable problems that dogged my existence, I was to all intents and purpose a totally different man.
The experience of winning the money, falling totally in love and losing it all within weeks had been the catalyst for a life change. Yes, it was a horrible experience but it led to a far greater life. Those I did tell about the ability disappeared from my life faster than the jockey exiting from the saddle of my hopes and dreams. The solitude and the sound of silence became my comfort, John my one real friend and writing now my one true passion. I finished my writing for one evening exhausted. I went over to close the curtains and knocked over a file resting on the arm of the chair. The contents scattered everywhere. I was not amused and my first thought was to just leave it there, but the thought of waking up to that mess in the morning was enough to convince me to do it there and then. Whilst picking up the loose papers I noticed a card amongst them. It was Shileen's card, the one I had been given in the shop. Christ, I had forgotten all about that. Perhaps it was time to ring her? The following day I telephoned. A very pleasant sounding voice said "hello, Shileen". "Hello, my name is Gary someone gave me your card. I'd like to know if it would be possible to see you?" "I am very busy, but perhaps someone will cancel and I can squeeze you in." I went on to explain a brief bit about my experience and then Shileen had a sudden change of heart. "I will fit you in next week" she said. "Great!" I replied.

We confirmed a time and date and the following week I turned up on her doorstep. I was greeted by the sight of hideous purple coloured door. I thought it was a dreadful colour and it certainly didn't help my sense of trepidation. I knocked gently and waited. The door opened slowly and there she was an attractive 40's something lady with strong features and eyes that looked like they could burn holes in snow. I felt somewhat intimidated by her powerful disposition, but her pleasant manner lifted my trepidation. The walls around her home were surrounded by Native American many pictures and artefacts. Shileen made some tea and then sat opposite me at a small table. She looked the part but I had not a clue what to expect. I was intrigued by what she would tell me, if indeed anything at all. She put my tea on the table and began to talk. "You have psychic abilities" she told me. "You also have healing hands". She also told me I was a channel for people in the spirit world? Psychic ability? Healing hands? Spirit world? Goodness! I was more confused than when I came in. Something had indeed happened to Dean that day with his left arm but could I really have healing hands? And was I in possession of genuine psychic ability? After an hour my head was swimming with all kinds of thoughts. I said my goodbyes to Shileen and thanked her. I sat at my table when I got home and got out my pen and paper and asked a question of John. "Was meeting Shileen all a waste of time?" Much to my surprise he told me Shileen was right. I did have psychic ability and healing hands and there was a 'Spirit world'. I was frankly astonished. There I am talking to a pen in my front room and having the audacity to think Shileen might be potty. In fact Shileen and I became friends for a short while

afterwards. What would my old friends from years back think of me now, if they knew I was in effect conversing with a pen? A cheap biro at that!
Oh well, I guess that was not important. I believed in what I did and believed it was true and that was all that really mattered. I realised voices in the head had a classified term in the medical profession, but I certainly wasn't suffering any mental health problems, well at least I thought I was of sound mental state. Now that I was hearing what I was about to write as a thought voice was much better. Having the words dictated to me was far better than just writing with no concept of what the next word would be. It really was like being a secretary, and writing the thoughts of someone who was dictating to you. I bought a couple of books about psychic ability to see if I could glean any understanding of what was happening to me and found there was something called 'Automatic Writing' where a spirit from the spirit world supposedly guides the hand of the channel and the writing appears on the paper, done at rapid speed, this was similar to mine with the rapid speed but I felt no controlling influence and indeed could stop and write at will. Even when the ability first came to me, I always felt in control rather than someone controlling my hand.
As explained earlier when I stopped writing so the message stopped, when I continued so did the message as you do when you're writing. From the beginning John had been a silent friend and all of a sudden his words were there in my head with great clarity. The ability to channel was becoming stronger everyday. Every now and again the voice would tell me something in the bathroom or the toilet, or just break in my own thought forms to relay a message when I least expected it.

It didn't always sound like John either, but it was difficult to be sure. I remember on one occasion being at a bus stop, when a thought voice in my head said as I looked at a very attractive girl in the queue "tell her Simon is no good." I trusted this thought voice message given to me and relayed it to the girl who said "I know I must get rid of him." She never even questioned my approach or how I knew Simon? It was totally bizarre, but these kind of things were soon to become commonplace. It was becoming apparent that I didn't need the pen and paper to relay messages which was an exciting new development. Things that Shileen had said weeks earlier had also began to make a little more sense. I was still open-minded as to whether I was in communication with the so-called spirit world, but it was beginning to seem a viable argument. After all what else could it be? Dead people talking? I know this sounds absurd; but do you have any better suggestions? It was beginning to sound more acceptable by the minute. At first it was quite difficult discriminating between my own thoughts and those of John, but I soon got the hang of it. I quickly was able to assimilate between the two. Not long after this I began to receive other voices of thought and these were clearly different from John and my own. It was astonishing! Sitting there writing the thoughts of others with just a pen. The thoughts being transcribed also were very different. As well as getting information relating to the past, present and future I was getting beautiful poetry and philosophy. In fact all manner of literature was dictated to me. I loved every minute of it. I began to put the works into files and was beginning to amass quite a collection. Almost everything told to me seemed to be of substance and very little of the material was banal. Although having said that, one or two of the authors of the material transcribed were certainly not Oscar Wilde and their material promptly hit the inside of the bin (no doubt causing consternation among them). There I was with little education being a critic! But even I was aware at this point of the good from the dross. I had a dictionary and became fully conversant with it, after having to look up hundreds of words that I had written. Many of those whose understanding I was unfamiliar with. For all I knew the words I was channelling may have been nonsensical and made the piece dictated meaningless, but time and again the words when I looked them up, they made perfect sense in the construction of the piece, I couldn't believe it. I would sit at the table with pen and paper then within a minute or two a wonderful piece of poetry or philosophy had been received. John was right I was being re-educated through the works. The voices that were channelling the material through me were succeeding in their desire, not only to have me write the stuff but be able to read, understand and enjoy it as well. I found that as the weeks progressed the thought voices became that much easier to pick up. It was rather like fine tuning a radio, the signal got stronger. Soon I was to have a reception loud and clear. It certainly was as John had said, they were re-educating me, but I wondered if that was its true purpose just re-education. As I grew more confident regarding the ability, it did become easier for me to talk about it and I became very open with it. Talking about the gift at this stage of my development was easier for me as my understanding was better, but for those I would talk to it obviously was extremely difficult to comprehend. It was part of me and I would declare

it so. No one I knew understood it or had a clue where the source of information was coming from apart from one, Shileen who at least appeared to have an understanding. So I decided at this point to try and find other interested parties. Who would understand something about psychic phenomena, the spirit world and what I was privileged too?
I was told by various contacts that a way to draw some understanding was to join a club or 'circle' where people there had similar experiences to share. Good idea! Maybe it was the right time to find others and share I thought. At last I made the relevant inquiries but felt the people I had met and spoke to were not for me, I had to be content with pursuing the road totally alone; gleaning what understanding I could from John and co. Even though I wrote reams of material, I never read books as such. Reading wasn't something of interest to me. My writings were much easier reading than any book and its information received totally absorbing and exciting, with its content an unknown commodity. So it was very interesting. You just never knew what the new day would open the mind to from one minute to the next. One day to another. Nobody knew what I would channel. It was always an air of 'expect the unexpected' and they didn't disappoint! And that is what made it so magical. You just never knew what you would be told. As the days flew by I became ever convinced that this intrusion in my life was for a specific reason. I did realise by this point I now had an obsession with the channelled writing and that it had began to dominate my whole existence. Perhaps this was not healthy? And the need to be more balanced would have been valuable advice. The writing just like the gambling had suddenly crept up on me and before I

knew it had become a part of me. At least with this obsession I was able to keep my blood pressure stable, my temper down, my migraine from appearing and what little I had in my pocket safe from those wretched bookmakers. I know it's a very difficult thing to comprehend so all I can do is demonstrate the ability and show some examples of the work.

Please note: All of the following material was channelled during the early stages of my journey in 1994. As with all the original pieces that were transcribed they were received at speed and without pause or grammar. The material I have transcribed through me you simply couldn't make it up could you? If so why would you want to? I know the truth and I know it is genuine but you as a reader can make of it what you will!

*A sample of some of the miscellaneous inspired Philosophical and other writings:*

*When learning of the spirit, one must learn of the soul. To know both is a blessed man. In knowledge one must attain a high standard of intellect to offer oneself to others. In wisdom one cannot give knowledge, but they can give the understanding in which wisdom is encased. The heart is full of tears and the head is full of nothing. When in life nothing has been learnt but suffering has filled ones soul.*

*The mind is the most deceptive of creatures.*
*Its understanding a complexity. And the acceptance of what constitutes reality is merely a perception that one deems a judgment.*

*I as a man of great intellect choose ones words carefully, whilst enjoying the finer elements of life. Must I say that to be a man of great wisdom, one must choose books in which they can grasp the words and indeed learn the meaning. I am withheld in my view that life is sometimes dull. But life when learning is never that.*

*One's mind is an eternal passage of knowledge. To understand the mind one must open it to the degree that the wisdom can be registered within. If the mind is wasted, then it continues to under-develop. It has such wonderful roads that are very rarely explored. Take to learning of wisdom; cram the mind full of literature, for tomorrow when one's mind is developed he shall teach.*

*How articulate is the man with the vast knowledge. One who can write words of such relevance. One who is truly blessed with words of great wisdom. Young man remember this, as a person who has been given such a remarkable gift, one is a highly privileged man indeed. As a man most truly blessed one must teach ones wisdom. One must act in true fellowship. One must endeavour to produce such works of inspiration.*

*When one of such unbelievable gift is given to this world, the world will take time to adjust. They will see, they will examine but how do they explain? In their sincerity they will concede defeat for they cannot begin to doubt. I shall bring forward my assessment of the gift by saying only a genius can understand, only a fool can disbelieve. Good day.*

*What if a man could see beyond today? What if a man could learn from one who has great understanding? A vast knowledge? A reason to believe? What if? What if no one can ever doubt? What if the world suddenly stopped to think could this be right? What if? What if no one could ever doubt? What if no one could ever question the existence of the afterlife? For surely this time is upon man. He can now see with his own eyes the afterlife writing, talking and giving help to those of earth time. Not what if but now!*

*Beyond the grave is from where we come. Beyond the grave do we speak. We bring tales and stories for human folk to read. We bring them love and romance. We bring them tales from our past and when you enter beyond the grave on the humans you have the last laugh. For they fear death. But how do I speak then? Give them this and enjoy!*

*For one whom sees there is no blindness.*
*For one whom hears there is no deafness.*
*For one whom learns there is no weakness.*
*For one whom is blessed, humbleness must be his friend. For one to learn he must listen well.*
*For one to teach he must have understood.*

*I concede that you young man have a mind so deep, it has no limits. It is a mind that has no boundaries. It is a mind that can search and find whichever it seeks. Your search for perfection will never be but your mind is an eternal river of thoughts.*

*The purpose of writing my dear boy is that you educate the mind. In the past many men have tried to write in inspired terms and have failed very badly. You are blessed with a gift in which you can write inspired at your leisure. It would appear to me that when one is tired one should rest. One like yourself has a twenty four hour gift, so why don't you rest at suitable hours? My dear boy spirit has been here long before you and will remain so long after your death. Please remember this I bid you good day!*

*The works you have just produced are the conclusion to your learning. All that is required now is to use the gift. To grow with the gift. To become the gift itself. The completion of the impossible. The completion of mind to eternal domain. To further the human brain to beyond tomorrow to the existence of the afterlife.*

Fear Not Young Man
the work is only just
beginning I have enormous
amounts to give You I will
Can Produce it or will
remember no one will
ever doubt what they
see and this Pleases
me immensely no one can
ever doubt where this
work has derived from
Its Value is immense Please
dear boy remember You
have endless endless
Material to write.

written 6 September
1994.

8 June 94 (72)

how Articulate is the Man
With the Vast knowledge
One whom Can Write Words
of Such relevence one
whom is truly blessed with
Words of great Wisdom
Young man remember this
has a Person who has been
given Such a remarkable gift
one is a highly Privaliged
Man and indeed one whom
Can Write with Such Integrity
is Indeed a man of great
Power I Shall leave you
with this thought young
man you Possess great
wisdom great knowledge
and great hindsight as
a man most truly blessed
one must teach one's wisdom
one must act in true fellowship
one must endeavour to Produce
Such Works of inspiration.

I Concede (35) that Man Many
Man have a Mind so
deep it has no limits
it is a Mind that has
no bandary it is a
Mind that can search
and find whichever it
seeks the Mind of a
truly great Man the
Mind of a genius Man
have been blessed with
the Mind and Soul of
a genius Man search
for perfection will never
be but Man Mind is an
eternal river of thoughts.

1 APR 94

I as a Man of
Great Intellect choose
ones Words Carefully
Whilst enjoying the
Finer elements of life
Must I say that to
be a Man of Great
Wisdom One Must choose
books in Which they
Can grasp the Words
And indeed learn the
Meaning I am Withheld
in My View that
life is Sometimes dull
But life when learning
is Never that.

12 JUNE 94

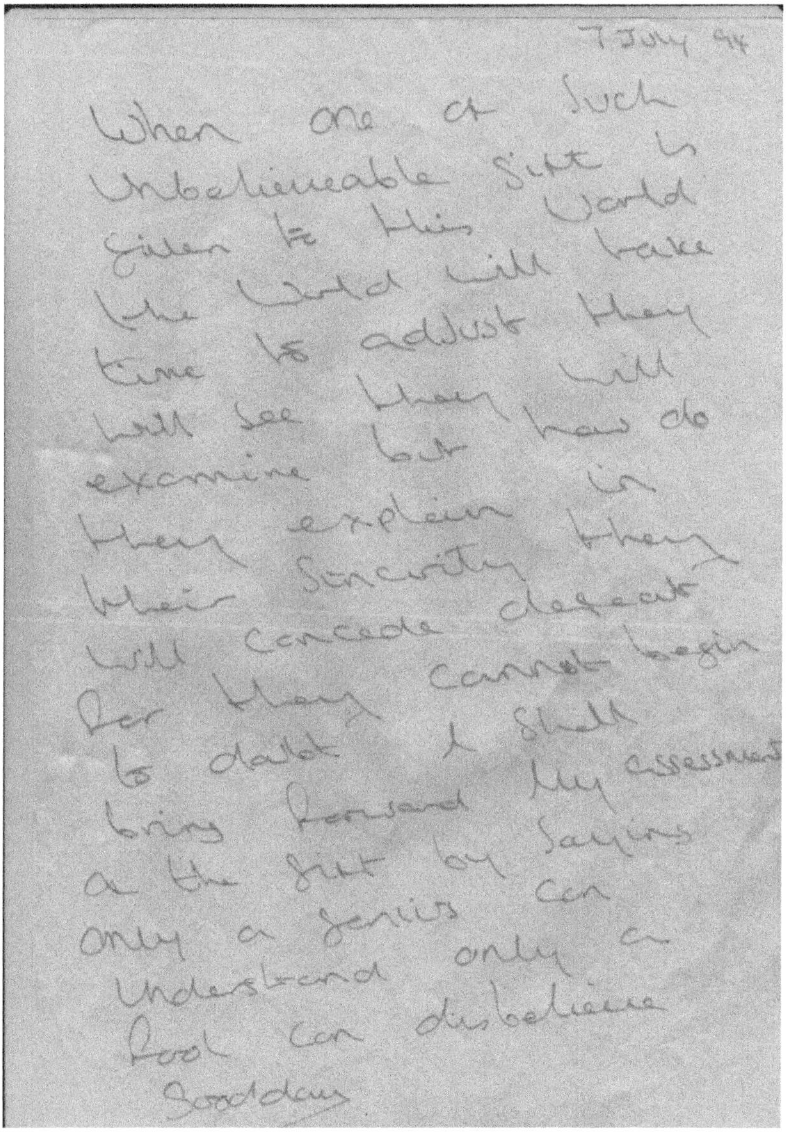

7 July 94

When one of such
Unbelieveable gift is
given to this World
the World will take
time to adjust they
will see they will
examine but how do
they explain in
their sincerity they
will concede defeat
for they cannot begin
to doubt I shall
bring forward my assessment
of the gift by saying
only a genius can
Understand only a
fool can disbelieve
Goodday

24 Jun 94

The Works You have
Just Produced are
the conclusion of
Your learning all
that is required now
is to use the gift
to expand on the gift
to grow with the gift
to become the gift
itself the completion
of the impossible the
completion of Mind to
eternal domains to
further the human brain
to beyond tomorrow
to the exsistence of
the here after.

23 June 94

Young Man You have every
Minute of every day to
enjoy the Works of Spirit
I trust You enjoyed the
Works Produced today every
Minute of every day
how Wonderful throughout the
Canvas Works You will astound
Many People with Your Sister
the Sheer brilliance of some of
the work to the Magnificent
Way in which You Produce the
article let no one doubt Spirit
for as time ends they to
will become as one they
Shall suffer what they did
only glory and love await
I Shall so Young Man
and Good luck.

8 June ?

The Purpose of writing
My dear boy is what you
educate the mind in the
Past many men have tried
to write in inspired terms
and have failed very badly
You are blessed with a gift
in which you can write
inspired at your leisure
it would appear to me that
when one is tired one should
rest one like yourself has
a 24 hr gift so why don't
you rest at suitable hours
My dear boy spirit as been
here long before you and will
remain so long after your
death please remember this
I bid you good day

 11-Sept 94

I would like to ask
you young man are you
enjoying your experience
of spiritual attainment
I believe you are sir
I believe you are sir you
is a wonderful gift you
possess and indeed are
a which defies understanding
use the gift well sir will
come as no surprise to you
that I am not a guide
but merely someone whom I
enjoys to write but I find
would say astounding and
your gift happens.
I know how it great pleasure
it gives me through you
in wanting to give you
I am able my
the benefit of under
lifetime I after
what it would be like

*Part one of two*

to be alive today but
in seeing some of the the
happenings throughout
I would say
wonder I'm not
I'm glad I'm
I would like you to know
that through my work
I gained immense satisfaction
and achieved relatively limited
success but you can through
the help of spirit achieve
enormous acclaim I honestly
wish you well and
hope all your dreams are
fulfilled you deserve
your success for your
tolerance and endeavour
can I just say on leaving
I wish you all the very
best.

*Part two of two*

If one is tired one should
rest one doesn't need any
Proof one doesn't need to
discover ones gift does
one Why does one need
to write endless Material
Please read dear boy
the rest is important
for a rested Mind is a
healthy Mind and one
which will Provide imaginative
and quality literature
to the tired Mind is
nothing but rest to the
healthy happy Mind is
Jayas information
Please rest
written Sept 1 1994

There is life after
death and there is
an eternity beyond
the grave. Spend no
time on fools for it
they don't believe you
with me. they never
will let the laughter
come from you not them
for you know the truth
let the fools believe in
nothing for surely they
will never have belief
if they doubt you

Saddam

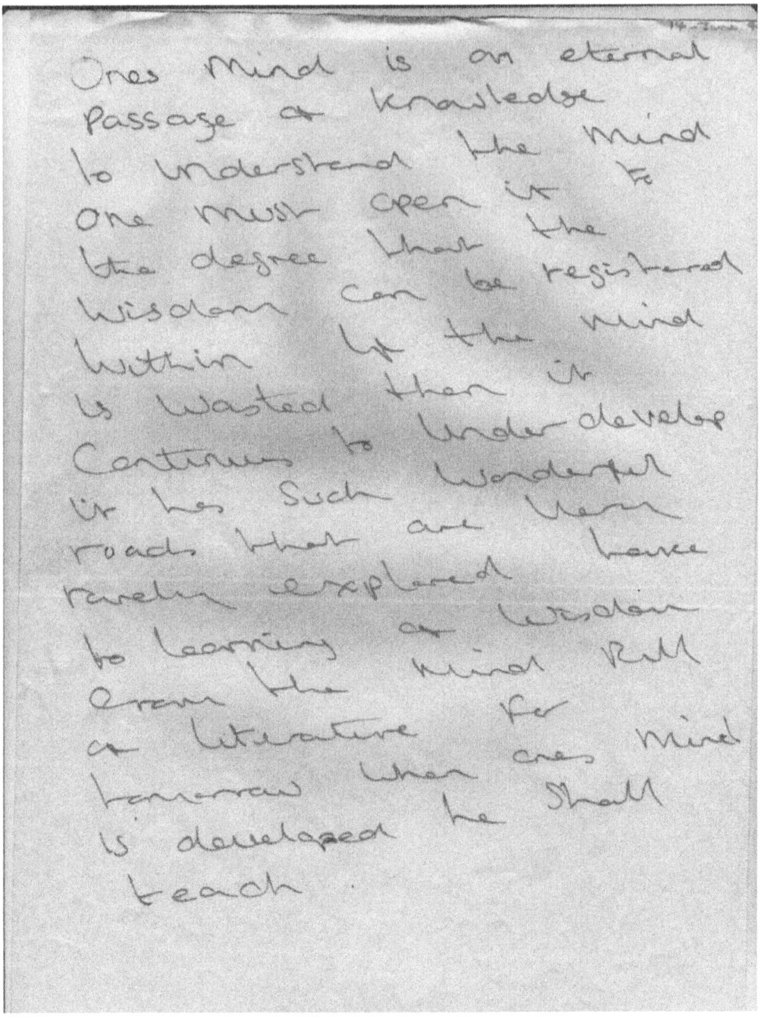
Ones mind is an eternal
passage of knowledge
to understand the mind
one must open it to
the degree that the
wisdom can be registered
within if the mind
is wasted then it
continues to under develop
it has such wonderful
roads that are them
rarely explored hence
to learning of wisdom
mind will
crave the
a literature for
tomorrow when ones mind
is developed he shall
teach.

*I believe the above writings are impossible to dispute when proper analysis is made. They clearly show evidence of the afterlife in communication with me.*

Being a Capricorn, stubbornness is a trait, and despite many kind words, and promptings for me, from my family to turn my back on John and return to a 'normal' existence, I just couldn't. It became a passion. Before I knew it months had passed since John first came into my life giving me his thoughts. I was leading a monk like existence. No sex, no fun, four walls for company, undergoing a total restructuring of my mindset. Experiencing such incredible emotion, that would roll up and down with passing each day. I was struggling to cope with the immense burden of being two people and with a comfort and despair of mind. Oh how I craved for some balance. A strong man made weak by the vice of self destruction in the gambling. Not even the sound of joyous laughter bridged the divide between me and pain. An afternoon of nags capitulating, smoke filled bookmakers with people inside who had spent their lives dreaming the impossible dream! And appearing to say here mate join the fu***** rest of us, be a loser, a dreamer. How I feel for those people who perhaps have ruined not only their own lives, but their families in the process. Boy, what a reality check that is! After my mood had subsided from its darkest despair it lightened the following morning on the receiving of my mail. A cheque from someone I had only met once. It was such a kind gesture. Amazing how money can make a very depressed soul feel as if life is just fantastic! It really helped me out. Filled with this joyous news I sat and talked to John again. "Gary" he said, "today you are to travel to Southend, a seaside town in Essex." "You are to leave soon after twelve o'clock." Oh no I thought… what about the racing? I will miss it. "There is someone for you to meet."

I sat pensive awaiting my instructions to unravel. John went on “there is a ship just outside of this place. The place you are to find is a public house and we have a name for you, Maureen. You will see on your arrival, the place will be quaint inside. There will be items around the interior taken from sea ships, many varied items.” I asked John if he could give me the exact whereabouts of this public house and information on Maureen. But he replied that my task was to find out. What Pratt is going to drive on a twenty mile round trip to a place he barely knows, looking for a public house whose name he doesn't know? You guessed it, me!
All kinds of thoughts entered my mind. What if I go all that way and there is no such place? Or what if I do find it and there is no one there? If there is, how the hell will I explain it all when I get there?
I tried to think about the message logically, which in the context of what was happening wasn’t very easy. The big question was whether to go or not?
A big dilemma! But if I believed in John and his messages, I just had to. If it were wrong, what would that then mean? A 20 odd mile trip, for nothing! £5.00 in petrol but worst of all I couldn't trust the information being given? What a blow that would have been, denting my un-floundering belief.
I am no detective but armed with a map, faith and my piece of written text given by John, I headed for Southend. The place I was seeking logically had to be by the sea, and so I headed there. The seafront at Southend is quite expansive. I was pleased as it was a pleasant day but not too warm. I remember thinking how quiet it was. It was pretty sparsely populated that day. At the height of summer it would have been very busy, making my task a little more difficult. I walked along looking at every

signpost, board or advertisement I could find. Nothing resembled in the slightest John's description, but patience is a virtue so they say and I had only been looking about ten minutes after all; so give it time I thought. Just then I came across 'The Ship' public house. This can't be it surely? It wasn't! It was rather large outside and as I popped my head through the door it was rather large inside as well. Slightly peeved with what had seemed a fruitless journey, I spoke to the only person on view and that happened to be the barman. I asked him if he knew the place I was looking for from any of my details on the paper I had just handed him? "Yes" he said. "That is my father's pub. Its 200 yards or so. On the left." Well, I couldn't believe my ears? I was astounded. I was very excited and I almost forgot to thank him as I hurried away. He had told me Maureen was the barmaid there, so if he was correct, this just had to be John's place of description. Arriving at the front door of the bar, I couldn't help but notice there was no ship outside. Laying that aside, I composed myself, and with some trepidation entered. Yes, the bar was small from the outside. Yes, it was quaint on the inside, and yes, there were items of a ship on the shelf around the interior of the place. 'My God' I thought, this is it. So case solved! This was John's destination, hallelujah! Now what? After glimpsing briefly around I walked towards the counter. The barman was briskly cleaning the glasses. I asked him if he knew of anyone called 'Maureen?' But how would I explain it all if I met her? Fortunately for me Maureen was on leave. Good I thought, perhaps it has saved me from some humiliating experience! (John had only told me to find the bloody place, but he didn't tell me what I would say when I got there?) Still, I was happy in the knowledge I had found it. This proved to me that listening to John was well founded. No Maureen, so now what? As I turned to leave I was asked a question by one of two women standing at the bar. They were in fact the only two people in there. They looked at me and one of them said "You're a medium." "No, I'm large!" (Old gag) "Yes, I am psychic, so I'm told". "Here is my card" She added. Well, I nearly died on the spot when she said, "I'm Frankie, and I am also psychic. I hardly ever come here for a drink in the daytime, so this must be fate" she added. "I have a message for you. You have a wonderful life. Read Ecclesiastes from the Bible, it will mean something to you at some point. Also read the book of Matthew." "I don't read the Bible" I replied. "I am being told to tell you Jacob's ladder. It will also have relevance to you in the future." She also went on to say "You are a Jesus like figure and have a wonderful life!" Goodness me, that is quite a statement! Sounded to me like complete nonsense. After a quick goodbye I left the pub totally dumbfounded. What an experience. I now knew the information I had received, was certainly the truth. But would Frankie's message have some future relevance? It taught me one lesson, that John and his friends from a world I couldn't see, smell or touch, but could only hear in minds thought, existed for certain. And with just a few words, could instigate something so unbelievable and magical. What Frankie had told me meant nothing at the time, but the fact of it was this was one hell of a day.

*Frankie's card*

I felt a new life just beginning. The odds of finding the place and meeting a psychic must have been millions to one. I could now finally believe that the communication was incredibly real and without question from an extraneous source that for many doesn't even exist. I for one began to believe in the existence of a 'Spirit World' I really did.

## CHAPTER THREE

### *PAINTING THE CANVAS*

As I sat in my front room watching a cat through the patio doors, I wondered what sort of day I would have. I then turned to the pages and pages of writings that stood before me. I was amazed by over the months how much I had actually produced. As I sat there I felt the need to pick up the pen again and as I wrote it read 'the heart is full of tears and the head is full of nothing, when in life nothing has been learnt but suffering has filled ones soul.' Bloody hell that's profound I thought. I had just finished the ending of yet another piece of philosophy from the authors from the Spirit World and I put the pen down. I then made myself a coffee and picked up the newspaper. Racing section, Newmarket on TV, Oh shit the first race has gone. Never mind I'll back a double. Bet is placed, chair adjusted, race is off. Seven furlongs of sheer hell as the Jockeys bustle for early position. Two furlongs out it's got a chance. One furlong out the whip is drawn, jockey moving up and down on the spot and the horse moving so fast backwards you could almost envisage it doing the milk round come morning. Bet gone west. You would have thought by now I would have learned wouldn't you? But like a fool I couldn't quite get the message. One minute thoughts like the Dalai Lama the next Joe mug the punter. What's the proverb easily parted a fool and his money. It hurt and it was devastating. Only a gambler can truly know the highs and lows.
The best description I could give of a punter like me is someone who enjoyed something so destructive.

Not a pot to p**s in, a head full of dreams and chasing a life changing win that never comes! Well not for me it didn't! But that's the problem with gambling, you win a small percentage but the big pot is always there tempting you. Everyday that's my last bet but the next day comes and it's same again please. God only knows why I put myself through it. But like all vices you have to touch rock bottom and then there is only one way up or one way out. It was sad how even having such a wonderful gift could not deter that demon inside from wanting to corrupt my saintly side.

The road I was travelling seemed to hit a dead end. Apart from the channelled writings it became a boring existence and it was just an existence. Life had become a monotonous treadmill. My writings were still coming through but life had very much stagnated. I had not had any words from John in recent times on a way forward. It was all becoming very frustrating, when out of the blue just like the message I had when I was told to go to Southend where I met Frankie the psychic, I received another message this time telling me to go to a place number 33 Belgrave Square. What's there I thought? I found out that it was the Spiritualist Association of Great Britain. John told me to go there before 1 pm. The time when I wrote the message was around 9.30 am, so I didn't have long before setting off as it was a two and a half hour journey. Now this really was a real test of my faith in it all. John said "there you will meet someone and you will know by this evening that it is." Hope it's a bird I thought (Maybe the girl of my dreams perhaps?). After getting ready I left and arrived after some delays just before one. Stepping inside the front door of what looked like from the outside a huge house, my sight was greeted by a counter on my right and a person behind it, who for some unknown reason seemed ill at ease by my presence. Just then two ladies entered the room. Two attractive ladies and twins to boot! Goodness me this is divine not one, but two! Miracles do happen! I stood browsing at some leaflets on my left and then they approached me. This is getting better I thought! We began to chat and they asked me if the resident psychic was any good? "I couldn't tell you, but I possibly can tell you what you need to know though? I have some psychic ability." I told them a couple of things which they appreciated. "They have a canteen just downstairs." said one of the ladies! "Great, well let's go then" they said. We arrived at the canteen and I asked "What would you like ladies?" "One tea no sugar and a tea for me one sugar, please." As we turned to find a table to sit at, I looked to see if anybody there took my eye as a possible candidate for John's message. Or could it have been the ladies I had just met? Alas there were no more pretty females other than the two sisters I had just met, but there was a distinguished looking man who appeared to be in his early seventies. With his silver hair, his build large and his looks that of a handsome rogue yep, I bet it's him! Just my bloody luck! After some prompting from one of the ladies I had just met I asked if we could join him. I felt a bit awkward but she gave me a gentle shove. "Sorry, would you mind if we sat here." "Not at all old boy" he replied. At that point I heard a voice in the confines of mind say "Gary tell him Ulla." "Who's Ulla" I blurted out. "Oh my God! How did you know my wife's name" said the gentleman.

He looked in a state of complete shock. "I don't really know to be honest" I said. "I just get the thought and sometimes the thought gives me names, places, messages etc." "That's amazing!" he said. Just then his eyes welled with tears. "My Wife Ulla died some 16 months ago. I can't believe you got her name, it was made up by her family for goodness sake." "Have I ever met you before?" "Did my wife ever meet you before?" said a disbelieving Ron. "Definitely not" I told him. He gave me his card. Ronald Bailey it read. "Nice to meet you Ronald, I'm Gary." I shook his hand and knew that my illusion of meeting a pretty female was shattered. It was this man I had been sent here to meet. F**k it, I thought just my luck! We decided we would all go and see the resident medium and after an hour left. I shook his hand. He smiled as we walked in opposite directions. I remember the two ladies dropping me off on my way home. I never saw the ladies again after that day but I was eternally grateful to them, for without them? Who knows I may not have talked to Ronald? A week after Ronald and I first met he called. I wasn't at all surprised as John had confirmed Ronald was the person I had to meet that day. We spent well over an hour on the telephone. It felt so right and he invited me over to his home in Harrow the following week. That week went so fast and the next minute there I was standing on Queensbury station in Harrow, on a bright sunny day, about to meet Ronald for the second time. Fully aware, unlike Ronald, that our meeting was destiny.
I arrived at Ronald's house in plenty of time.
His home, a smallish two-bedroom house crammed with antiquities. He led me through to his front room. It was a room full to the brim with books of

all descriptions. "My wife read everything" he said. We sat and talked about almost everything under the sun. Our day was superb and just as I had hoped, a new friend had been found and a new road of which where it would lead I knew not. A few weeks later Ronald and I were the best of friends. Ronald treated me like the son he never had and for me, Ronald, apart from being a man I loved dearly was also my ears when no one else would listen. I spent hours on the telephone to him talking predominantly about the works I had transcribed that day among many other things. He was a great conversationalist. Ronald loved the chats and the philosophy although he was a bit of a diplomat at times and when he didn't like something that had come through he would say "that's interesting, um, interesting". I often thought (you lying b*****d). The word 'interesting' said in a long drawn out way. That old goat could charm the knickers of a Nun! Such was his silver tongue and his extensive use of the English language. He was a real life cad. An English gent with the kick of a mule but I had the greatest respect for him. He was also told me he was an RAF boxing champ in his day and was very proud of his boxing ability. Age had not dented his extreme pride. After a few months of endless banter and dialogue Ronald told me how incredible he found my ability. He also admitted he had tried to find a flaw in everything I said and did as regards the channelling, but finally had to accept that although it was beyond his concept of understanding (mine too!) there was no flaw. Whatever had brought us together had certainly been inspirational, not only for me but for Ronald himself. After meeting Ronald my channelled writings certainly became more profound.

*Ronald Bailey*

I soon had hundreds of writings. The intellect and personality of the poems were all very different. All the poems are original as are the other philosophical writings. I met Ronald in the summer of 1994 and it was shortly after meeting him that my writings began to change. I was still producing the odd piece of philosophy and poetry when then come a different form of writing. A language that was totally alien to me. The words I was now hearing in the confines of mind were Thee, Thou, Hast, Hath, Beauteous, etc. I frankly didn't have a clue what they meant. The words as before were given to me in thought form and written down.
The spelling though was a real problem. Unlike before when I could just pick up the dictionary for help with a word. With these words many were not even in the dictionary. I wrote them as I thought they sounded but sometimes Thee, Thy, Hast and Hath became a little confusing and I wrote them

down wrongly and the piece wasn't right in its construction. Ronald understood a little as regards the old English and pointed out the obvious mistakes. Thee, Thy, Thou, Hast, Hath and many others were similar sounding words and it was a nightmare at first but I persevered as best I could.
I was writing pieces of work that were completely nonsensical to my understanding. I telephoned Ronald and asked him what he thought of the new writings that had just come through. As I read the first of three pieces he was very quiet and non-reactionary. Normally he would be critical or full of praise but this time he remained silent. "Are you ok Ronald?" I said worryingly." "Yes, I am just so shocked, astounded even! I can't believe the stuff you are writing. Where does it all come from for God's sake?" "Search me" I replied. "Some of the words are not quite in the right place in the context of the piece, but it seems wonderfully good stuff.
I know couldn't write it and I don't think you could either" he said. He added "It is very difficult to comprehend Gary." I agree totally Ron it is."
"I know the words are from Shakespearian times. They are olden day English. Let me find my book of Shakespeare sonnets for you. I will read you something." "Hang on Ronald whose is Shakespeare?" "What the hell is a sonnet?" I really hadn't a clue! Ronald couldn't believe I had never heard of Shakespeare, especially as I was near 34 at the time. He left me hanging on the other end of the line for a few minutes before he returned.
"Now dear boy, this is Shakespeare sonnet 144."
He went on to read the opening lines and something stirred within me. I went cold. "Stop Ronald" I said.
"I must find out more about this Shakespeare for myself" and with that we ended the conversation.

Shakespeare? Who was he? And just what had stirred within me when Ronald read sonnet 144?

***Shakespeare's Sonnet 144***

*Two loves I have of comfort and despair,*
*Which like two spirits do suggest me still:*
*The better angel is a man right fair,*
*The worser spirit a woman colour'd ill.*
*To win me soon to hell, my female evil*
*Tempteth my better angel from my side,*
*And would corrupt my saint to be a devil,*
*Wooing his purity with her foul pride.*
*And whether that my angel be turn'd fiend*
*Suspect I may, but not directly tell;*
*But being both from me, both to each friend,*
*I guess one angel in another's hell:*
*Yet this shall I ne'er know, but live in doubt,*
*Till my bad angel fire my good one out.*

*Sample of the channelled poetical works taken from my book Dead Poet's Pen...*

*Astronomy Speaks*

Most beauteous the stars, astronomy speaks. Heavens abide the twinkled dust. Eternities roll Thy favoured tongue. Disenchanted arrows of Petulance rear a cankered head, embarking a Density of ignorance, wherein celestial orbits Rise and fall. Piteous thy mind, where visions Deem thy sight an erroneous intrusion. Seek Thy setting sun and fleeting thy vision, where Glorious beams of light do descend from heavenly spheres, Embracing solitude and harmony forthwith and Yet in persuasive eye do pry the substance of The soul. Wishing thy travels ascend to Beyond thy visionary sight, to fields of stars And a rolling universe beyond thy mind.

*Lost In The Winds That Blow*

Though young am I and fortunes fade this Hour, this day, I lay fallen with friends I barely Know. Such is this war, oh lovely war, where Numbers not names have meaning. Dreams Lay scattered in fields, with fires burning into The night. Wretched war, that cursed war that Scars the heart. Bemoan a soldier's life.
A worthy man, but a worthless corpse, in Bloody fields far from home. Where is the Reason? Where is the hope? When letters to Love ones penned, lay muddied, lost in the Winds that blow. War in anyone's name? Not Mine or yours!

*A Painting of Life*

I painted the picture of life.
I used images in my mind.
I used colours to portray emotion.
I used strokes that move in time with the
Days of life. I used mirrors that reflect the
Image in The face of the tired man. I used
Conundrums to fill the minds of those whom
Search the painting. I used degrees of self to
Portray my picture. The picture a painting of
Life.

*A Letter to Marilyn Monroe*

Who could have ever dreamed of the life you
Would have. A babe to a beauty, unknown to
An idol. Who truly knew you, the Hollywood
Star? Who could have loved you more than the
Millions now? I think I kind of knew you,
Somewhere in my distant past, a girl with a
head full of dreams. Where love deserted you,
Hope never did. Where pain tortured and
Racked you, hope never did. Where too many
Judged you without care or remorse. Marilyn
Monroe, we knew only a shadow of what you
Were. Tears wore like a mask where only your
Smile could deceive. I think that I love you now.
I think that I loved you then. Love, sweet
Marilyn, that was you. You were so funny and
Bright too. Not at all dizzy, oh no, not you!
Beauty personified. Man's perfect dream.
No one could doubt you were a star in all
Scenes. All that we are left with is all that you
Were. Love, beauty and a star in an uncaring
World.

*In the following pages you will see some original untitled poetical works as they were written, at speed and without punctuation or grammar. Please note: for clarity purposes I do not claim the works to be from any famous dead poets Shakespeare or otherwise but from unknown sources.*

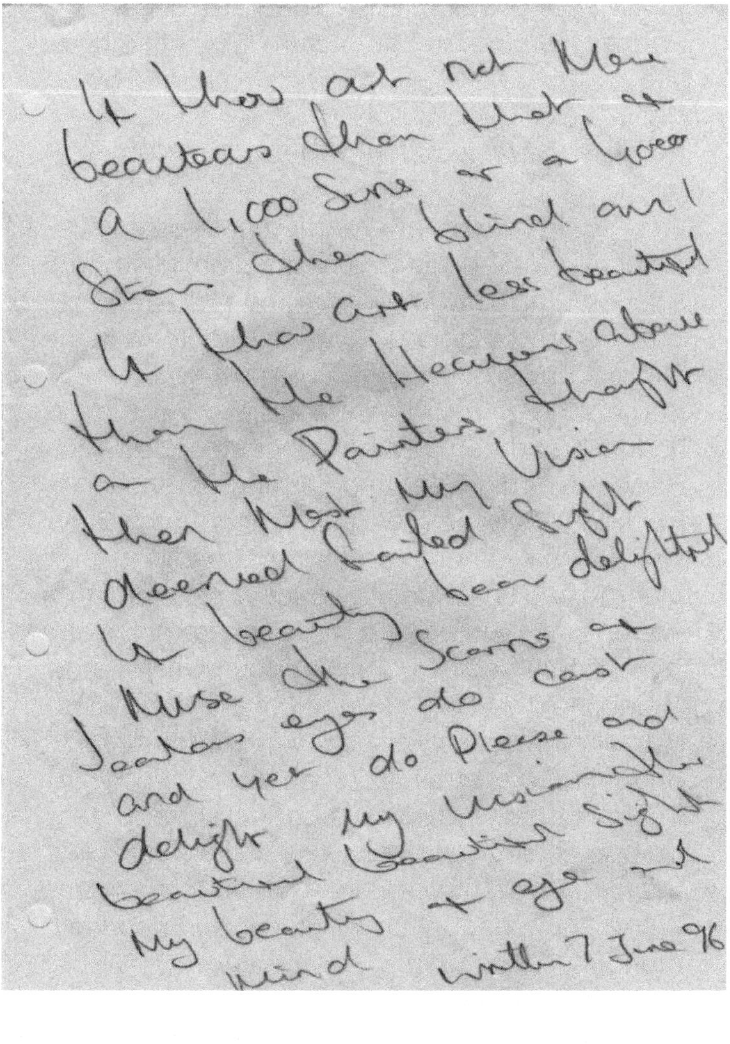
If thou art not More
beauteous than that of
a 1,000 Suns or a 1,000
Stars then blind am I
If thou art less beautiful
than the Heavens above
than the Painters thought
or the Painters Vision
then Most my Vision
deemed failed sight
thy beauty been delighted
Muse the Scorns of
Jealous eyes do cast
and yet do Please and
delight my vision the
beautiful beautiful sight
My beauty of eye and
mind written 7 June 96

I Painted the Picture
of life I Used Images
in my mind I Used
colours to Portray emotions
I Used Strokes that mark
in time with the days
a life I Used Mirrors to
reflect the Images in the
face of the tired man
I Used Conundrums to fill
the Minds of those who
Search the Paintings of life
I Use degrees of self to
Portray my Picture
The Picture a Paintings of life.

11 Nov 94

My despairing conscience
torn in two evading
truth and finding
irrelevance a sordid
friend perpetual deviance
soiling a mind weakened
pitied am I to chose
between a conscience
soiled and truth pervade
dignity
me a tolerance of
perusing a mind of
indifference perceive
in minds eye a tolerate
side a conscience to
truck but woe is me
his time of madness
melancholy me and a
conscience soiled.

13 Jan 95.

Methinks time the
Dial of day speeds
Word, a loneliness
Words of disdain
Inappropriate Words ill
Work on this day
a day of despair
my conscience plays
a sombre time of
which I sigh this
day I cry a tear
seek sadden
that
longing despised
each word that
descends time methinks
day must time to
night for sigh to
him to sleep to
dream forgotten day
and time of clean

O Conscience be thy
Guiding light but thou
An Illusion in this hour
Night forbidden to speak
for fear of offend
O Conscience be thy Guide
To speak not doth make
My Anger rage whence
thy imagine a gentleman
blade that cut thy
Conscience into two
fear anger retorted
view at degrading mind
thus to find thy
conscience doth reside
to which side that
show so hard to please
Conscience or which I
heed your Judgement

24 June 75.

Though Young am I
and fortunes fade so
Quickly his hour, His day
I lay fallen with,
friends I barely knew
Such is this War
Oh lonely War where
number nor names have
Meaning. Dreams lay
Scattered in fields with
fires burning into the night
Wretched War that cursed
War what scars the heart
Bemoan a soldiers life
a worthless man but
worthless corpse in
the bloody fields far from
Home where is the
reason where is the hope

The Poppy a symbol of
a human's greatest sacrifice
death
They that give their life
for a cause worthy or not
let or never be forgotten
that the life lighter gears at
a life if one has given
it for that which they
truly believe the Poppy shall represent
them—
it is the flower which grows
where no one knows
A symbol of mankind's eternal
memory you have not the
beauty of the Rose or
the sweet smell of the

*Postcard from the late Singer/Actor Anthony Newley who I had the privilege to meet backstage at his last appearance at the Green Room, Regent St in London. I also met actor David Soul there too!*

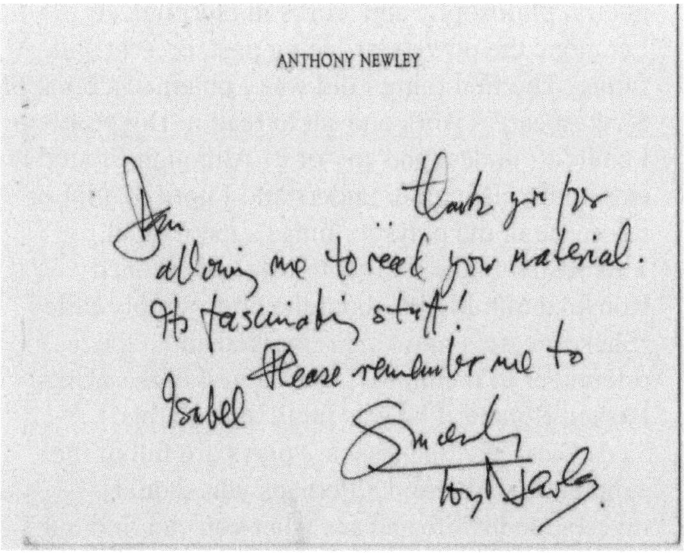

ANTHONY NEWLEY

[illegible] .. thank you for
allowing me to read your material.
Its fascinating stuff!
Please remember me to
Isabel
Sincerely
Tony Newley.

*"Thank you for allowing me to read your material. Its fascinating stuff!" - Anthony Newley*

I retired early to bed with a head full of thoughts and an excitement I hadn't felt before. I came to the conclusion that I was definitely being re-educated and for some purpose. What other reason could there be for these voices of thought giving me poetry, philosophy and works in old English?
Let alone the powers of seeing past, present and future. The first thing I did was I obtained a book of Shakespeare's work and sat to read it. Big problem, I couldn't understand any of it! Although I found it extremely difficult to understand I noticed a lot of reference in the plays to things supernatural.
This really grabbed my interest. I telephoned Ronald and told him about the book simply called 'Shakespeare's plays'. I remarked about the references to the things supernatural in the works.
I asked Ronald if he was familiar with this.
"Yes Gary, the Shakespeare plays are full of the supernatural" he said. "Perhaps you should investigate his life and see what you can find out?"
"My wife was always on about paranormal things but I thought she was completely mad and now you, perhaps I'm the mad one? (Laughing out loud)."
"Why don't you come over and look through Ulla's old books? Perhaps you'll find something.
She collected books on everything." "Good idea" I said "I will come and see what I can find."
Three days later it was back to Harrow. I found myself rummaging through Ronald's front room making an assault on Ulla's books. "Anything you find if you want it, it is yours" said Ronald.
"Great!" I found a number of interesting books.
An original book of Cristina Rossetti poems, a book of poetry by American Ella Wheeler Wilcox, a book of Queen Elizabeth the first and a couple of books

on psychic phenomena. My hands were like magnets where these books were concerned. It seemed so strange how I felt drawn to only certain, specific books. I sat at Ronald's table, flicked through them. It was then I came to the life story of Queen Elizabeth the first. My history was poor, so I had no idea why I should be so drawn to this book in particular. I then became aware that I was being drawn to certain lines and certain words in the book and one name appeared to leap at me from the page a Dr Dee. A Dr John Dee. What was Dr Dee all about? I wondered. Why had he been drawn to my attention? I thought perhaps it was best to do some research on Dr Dee. At least while researching this, the gambling would be restricted and thoughts of browsing through the runners and riders would take second place. Ronald made some lunch and we had some very entertaining banter when I started to feel the need to write. Ron said all he had was some odd pieces of paper or some envelopes, so I said that would do me. He gave me a pen and I started to channel some poetic works. One poem caught the eye because it talked about a crested lark as being a beautiful songbird. I asked Ron who sat there watching me write quickly if he knew of such a bird as the crested lark. "No, I love the poem, but does the crested lark even exist?" said Ron. He told me to look amongst Ulla's books to see if there were any bird books. As I reached up onto the top shelf I spotted a book called Rare European Birds and when we searched the books contents, sure enough we found a page all about the crested lark which is now sadly extinct, but it was a beautiful songbird. This proved to Ron that the information I had just channelled in front of his eyes was as I had previously said from some extraneous source and certainly not my own thought process. He was gob smacked. Another poem I have mentions an extinct fly called a 'Tansy' and it is impossible I could have known of this, or indeed read of this at anytime or anywhere in my life. This I think convinced him more than anything of the genuineness of the gift! "Why don't you stay over tonight?" (a voice breaking my deepest thought) "Why not, thanks Ronald" I replied. It was late anyway and I was tired and the thought of travelling home was not seducing my thoughts. "You can sleep down here in the front room Gary as Ulla's room is crammed full of all kinds of things and until I get the chance to clear it, it is just not possible to get in there at the moment." "Sh*t" I thought it's going to be bloody cold down on the floor, but still I'm tired, it's a long way home and Ronald has kindly offered, so yes, I'll stay. We made a makeshift bed on the floor and the lights went out. That night I was to get one of the biggest shocks of my life. It was pitch black. I closed my eyes and fell fast asleep. It wasn't too cold really, though hardly five star. I was awoken in the early hours. Finding myself sat bolt upright, looking up at the ceiling as the vision of a head floated by. The head (at least that was all I could see) was that of a beautiful woman. Early thirties, fifties style hair fashion with a serene smile. She looked down upon my mortified body with its heart pounding beneath its T-shirt. The head appeared to float towards the door from the centre of the room and promptly disappeared. I was astonished. I wanted to call Ronald but simply couldn't. The next thing I knew it was morning. I was awoken this time by Ronald's loud raucous cough.

“Good morning dear boy” he said. “Ronald you won't believe this” relaying the story to him of the ghostly vision. He listened intently to the story and without a word reached to the top shelf where he took a photograph down and handed it to me. “Was this her?” he asked, It was! I could hardly believe it. “Yes Ron, that’s the person I saw last night.”
“Oh my God,” he said as he sat hands cupped over his face. He looked absolutely stunned. He knew I had never seen his wife Ulla, not even a picture and yet from the accurate description I had given him of the vision he knew it was his wife. When Ronald had composed himself, he like myself, wondered why the vision was of someone young and beautiful. When Ulla died she was very thin, frail and terribly ill and more importantly over 60 years old. In the vision she was early thirties. It was mind-boggling. It added another dimension to my understanding. My vision had meant I not only had a possible communication with life after death through the writings, but also I had actually seen the distinct probability of life after death with my own eyes. Was I in communication with people long dead? The jury was out on that one, but I had no logical explanation to it and I was sure Ronald didn’t either, as he remarked “I saw almost everything conceivable in the war but nothing compares to what I have seen since we met. The insight you have given me over these past few months has been truly remarkable.” How wonderful to get the name Ulla to give to Ronald and then some months later have the vision of her as proof of life after death! “It’s not me Ron, is it?” I replied. “I wish I knew” he said, “I wish I knew.” I left that morning wondering whether I should have disclosed my vision to Ronald in view of how shocked he

was, but I realised the vision was for him just as much as for me. I knew that no matter what anyone else said or thought, my vision would stay with me forever. Life after death was not only possible in my eyes, it was highly probable.

# CHAPTER FOUR

## *SHAKESPEARES GHOST*

I became fascinated with Shakespeare as a subject matter after seeing the vision of Ulla, because Shakespeare talked much of ghosts etc in his works and having seen a ghost myself, it suddenly made it all the more realistic. It occurred to me on browsing Shakespeare's works that he like me had a total fascination with the paranormal. After seeing the dead wife of Ronald that night I had no doubt of the existence of ghosts, so to me the stories throughout Shakespeare of ghosts were very real and not some figment of great imagination. I became fascinated by Shakespeare the man but found nothing about him quite added up. His life was an enigma from what I could make out. Something puzzled me greatly about the Shakespeare story I just couldn't fathom out quite what it was. I gave up racking my brain at this point and took a bus ride to Basildon town centre. I popped into the local library and asked if they had any books on Shakespeare or Dr Dee. I discovered there was much on Shakespeare but virtually nothing on Dr Dee. In fact I would have to wait for a book on Dee as the only one available would take a couple of weeks to obtain. It has to be ordered. Ok I thought no problem I will get it anyway. I ordered the book which was called 'The Private Diaries of Dr Dee'and left. My life was suddenly taking a very exciting turn. I felt like a detective on a mission, only no crime to investigate! Well, hopefully not!

*Elizabethan Astrologer Dr John Dee Ashmolean Museum*

*William Shakespeare*

It was all a very exciting adventure, with me hoping that I might be unearthing something rather magical. My head was somewhat in the clouds as I strolled through the town centre until the next thing I recall was seeing a large sign outside of the hairdressers. I noticed the sign because it wasn't just offering cuts or blow drying but tarot reading. That's unusual … so I decided to have a look and see what it was all about. On entering the shop some attractive females caught my eye, but my hopes of it being one of those darlings reading the cards were dashed when I asked 'Tarot reading?' Only to be greeted by a voice straight from the boots "upstairs, tarot reading, mate!" said a gravelled voiced old lady having her blue rinse done. I walked up some stairs on my left and entered a room on the landing at the top. "Be with you in a minute love" said a lady, head appearing from behind a curtain. 5 minutes later the curtain opened fully and the lady introduced herself. "Hi, I am Marion what can I do for you?" We talked for a short time and I told her of my strange experience "fantastic!" she said "my friend would love to meet you, her name is Gwen and she channels as well, but her gift is singing." "Great, I would like to meet her." We then exchanged numbers and Marion told me to come back on the Wednesday morning which I did. It was there I met Gwen who was dressed in flamboyant mauve. She was an amazing lady. After a couple of hours of non-stop chatting I gave her my telephone number. I asked her to call me and to come over one evening to look at the material I had channelled. Gwen told me she had written a book called 'Russell' the story of her young son who sadly died. Gwen told me she totally believed in life after death because of her experiences. "Yes, I will come over" she said and true to her word she did. The problem with me at that stage in my life was I tried to cram all my experiences into any one conversation I had, so I must have rattled on like a demented parrot. I would describe myself like a coiled spring that would explode into conversation about me and the gift every time I got the chance. I never talked to anyone about the gift only Ronald, so when I got the chance to unleash the beast it was the full Monty. Oh those poor people who had to listen to it! Gwen visited me days later with a couple of friends (one of those friends Tony Stockwell has become quite a famous psychic celebrity these days) he was unknown then, but I told him he would be famous and years later so he is! We had a most enjoyable evening. During the visit we tried a couple of psychic experiments. In one of those experiments a candle was placed in front of me and the room was darkened. Gwen, Stockwell and his friend sat staring intently at me. Gwen said she saw a couple of spirit faces that appeared to her, which were apparently with me (I believe this is called transfiguration). The friends with her also saw these faces and described them, exactly as did Gwen. It was bizarre. I never doubted what they said they had seen, but kept an open mind. Two weeks later a phone call came from a very excited Gwen. A friend of hers in Hertfordshire had sent her some drawings that very morning, these drawings were of the very faces that Gwen and her friends had seen that evening at my house, it was remarkable. Gwen sent me those drawings and they did look remarkably similar to their description of the faces they had seen that night. I wrote and thanked Geraldine the lady who had sent the pictures to Gwen. There were so many extraordinary things happening by now that if I hadn't seen them and experienced them for myself I would never have believed it possible.

*Could this be a channelled drawing of John?*
*by Geraldine R.*

*Another channelled drawing of a spirit face that was witnessed by Gwen Byrne & Tony Stockwell.*

Gwen left my life almost as quickly as she had entered it, but not before introducing me to one of her closet friends Deborah. I met Deborah briefly over a coffee and had hoped a new friendship would be formed, but alas this was not to be, but a letter she was to send me would truly begin my search. In her letter she told me that she had channelled a message but did not understand it, although she was certain it was for me. This message had apparently come from a group of spiritual masters called

'The Great White Brotherhood' of which Jesus is supposed to have belonged. I didn't personally believe in Jesus but kept an open mind.

The message read:

*'Where the white swan glides queen of all the birds, there and there alone you will hear our words, at last when the white swan joins you to sail along your way. Then our words will truly be spoken and love will find a way' signed Alpha, Omega.*

What a strange message I thought and who or what is this Swan? I wasn't interested in religion or the Bible at all, so the Jesus bit left me baffled, but still being open minded I took it in without allowing myself to become convinced that the letter was for me. I never saw Deborah again but kept the letter safe and I remembered the words of that message. I kept thinking about the swan and what was the Great white brotherhood? The mystery was all set to deepen.

Ronald and I were still enjoying a wonderful friendship and he invited me to meet a friend of his, a delightful chap called Julian. Julian lived and worked at a horse riding stables in Harrow. I arrived at the entrance to the stables to be greeted by a vision of complete splendour. Acres of wonderful woodland, it was like something out of Dallas that television series from the eighties. You must also bear in mind I was totally uncultured and hadn't seen luxury in any capacity, apart from the soap you buy which has luxury written on it! The East End is a little devoid of luxury, well at least the bit I knew was. Ronald introduced me to Julian, he of the highly eloquent accent and debonair mannerism, to me of the not so eloquent manner and the 'wash the mouth out with soap' cockney wide boy character. One could say a complete meeting of minds? Methinks not! However; I think he warmed to me slightly, it was a bit like posh and dosh meets mouth and wash! Well you get the gist of things don't you? "Ronald has told me a lot about you Gary, sounds fascinating. Do you think that you could help my little dog with your healing gift? He has arthritis in one of his legs." "Let me show you him." He then introduced me to a beautiful, white Highland terrier type with the 'dog cost a bomb' look to it. Well-groomed, spoilt one would assume. "Give me her over here and I will have a look." Sure enough I picked the mutt up being gentle not to harm its leg as I took it in my arms and within seconds I put him down. Without thinking I had done anything to help the pampered pouch, off he ran as fast as a greyhound with an excited Julian saying it's a miracle, his leg is fine. Ronald was just as amazed "for God's sake the dog is fine." "Three years that dog has had a bad back leg, but it looks ok now. That is amazing!" "Thank you very much indeed" said Julian. I was dumbfounded, but if Julian and Ron were convinced something had happened that was fine by me! The same had happened with my friend Dean without even trying they seemed to be healed. Still shaken by the apparent miracle that had taken place we all went inside of his beautifully kept home and he sat at a piano. "Do you like Bach?" he added. Me trying to sound educated and cultured said, "Yes, love it!" thinking to myself who the f*** is Bach. He played a classical piece and I must admit it was rather beautiful, he then asked me if after tea if I would take a look at a couple of his horses that had problems. "Of course" I said. After tea he took Ronald and me to the stable area. "This one has back problems and this one is just under the weather I believe. Could you please try to help these two?" I gave both the horses healing and told Julian to let me know how it went. I left about five that evening feeling rather pleased with my day. Ronald promised to keep me updated. It had been a great adventure mixing with the upper classes. A perfect sort of day! No offer of any money mind! In fairness I think his mum treated us to a meal, so it wasn't all bad.

I loved the little train excursions they were fun. In fact a train journey to Essex brought my next surprise. I sat down in a rather busy carriage, opposite a blonde lady. My mind was wandering with all kinds of thoughts like (is she wearing stockings?) Oh well you know what men are like! When the words 'tell her Peter' came to mind. I ignored it the first time but again it came, tell her Peter. On the third occasion I asked the blonde lady if she knew Peter. "Yes, he is my boss!"(looking somewhat startled.) I explained I had some psychic ability and I had just been given a message to pass on to her. She explained to me her friend was also psychic. She gave me her business card and suggested we meet again. She left the train at the next stop. I remember thinking to myself how bizarre these 'meeting people incidents' were becoming. Were these people and I was destined to meet? On arriving home I telephoned Ronald to tell him of my strange experience on the train and to ask if he knew of any possible connecting factor between John Dee and Shakespeare. Ron said he had not even heard of John Dee. He also had no

news on the horses I gave healing either. Ron remarked he would telephone the stables at some point that day and to leave it with him and if he got any news he would get straight back to me.
After putting the phone down on Ronald a thought popped into mind to ring Margaret, the woman I met on the train. I went to my coat and got her business card and a few minutes later I telephoned her. The conversation flowed and we arranged to meet up a couple weeks later. Margaret unlike Ronald was more attuned to spiritual matters and talking to her about visions and channelling was much easier than it had been explaining it all to Ron when I first met him. I was sure I hadn't met Margaret for no reason and later in the story she was to prove very, very important to major events in my life. My channelled writings were at this point ever expanding. I was acquiring an enormous selection of very diverse material. The writings were changing in both quality and content from their humble beginnings. The thing I enjoyed most about the hours of channelling was that I never knew quite what would come through. One day it might be pages of philosophy, the next poetry and the next some conversational text regarding the future. Sometimes it was a mixture of many writings. It was tremendously exciting stuff. One thing it was never and that was boring. My mind was like a river of thoughts that never ran dry. Pick up the pen and you have lift off. My thoughts would never dry as it was an endless stream. If I wanted it was 24 hours a day on tap. Well as least the communication was if not the poetry etc. The gambling had fallen away a little at this stage but it could always raise its ugly head. There was no room for complacency but it seemed the meeting of new

friends etc helped me to focus my attention away from the jolly old nags. I never told my friends of my problem with gambling simply because I didn't think I had one. Being two people as I was at the time, with a side I liked and one I hated wasn't easy. The best of me surfaced when channelling and the worst when I was gambling. I suppose if I had never won the £19,000 it would have made the decision to stop a simple one, but the buzz when winning if only rarely, keeps you on a high and kept me near addicted. I was in my own little world most of the time, a slave to my pen and to my punting.

My growth at least in an educational sense was something quite special, it meant my mind didn't degenerate to the realms of race form and telling everyone how unlucky the nag was, who had just lost on the line emptying my pocket rapidly. Chasing losses? That's a bastard. Every gambler has done it. Lose £10, try to get it back, lose £20 and so on. A gamblers hard luck story is a tough one to endure. Oh those poor souls who daily endure it. Thank God for those voices in my head keeping me sane (now there's a novelty). I remember time had become a great irrelevance. Time no longer seemed significant to me. For me there was no time, only change. In my own little world I was oblivious to all around me, insulated in my comfort zone of pen and paper. Of course I had jobs of one sort or another to pay the bills but working with others not like minded was incredibly difficult. If only gambling could suffice and meant you didn't have to work? If you were good at it perhaps you wouldn't, sadly not one of my best attributes. That big old world kept on turning waiting for not man or beast. Time when I channelled just flew by. My muse was my friend. Only betting slips in-between kept me firmly on planet earth!!!

Having almost forgotten about Shakespeare and Dee, out of the blue a package arrived from Geraldine (the one who did the spirit drawings and friend of Gwen) accompanied by a nice letter.
I thought this could be useful to you she said. It was a book called 'The Shakespeare Conspiracy' by Graham Phillips and Martin Keatman. I was never one for reading a book, as previously mentioned and I found it hard to keep a concentrated effort for any length of time, but I did my best. Unfortunately three pages and the book went down. I couldn't for the life of me stay focused. As soon as I put the book down I picked up a pen and some paper and began channelling. I noticed part of the message being given to me was in relation to Shakespeare and how I needed to keep researching him as it was of the utmost importance to my path and another clue came in the form of 'all roads lead to France'.
I had this message before some weeks back and yet I knew no French people and the chances of me going to France were practically zero. I had absolutely no desire to go there. What could it possibly mean 'All roads lead to France?'
And what was this Shakespeare research for?
And just why did Geraldine send me the book called 'The Shakespeare conspiracy?' Just then the phone rang it was Ronald. "Ah Ron, I was just about to call you." "Gary, I've just come back from the stables (his voice lowered) you bloody marvel! The horses have shown signs of improvement. Julian can't thank you enough. In fact there is another horse and the owner has told me she will give you the world if you can help it with its eye

problem. She thinks the world of him and has heard about your work on the other horses and would like you to help. It's a great opportunity for you."
"Brilliant, that's fantastic." I replied. "It really worked then?" "Yes it did" said Ron. "Come over when you like to help the other one. I'm sure the lady will give you anything you want. She's very wealthy" he added. "Why not!" Next day I was up like a lark, no messing, clothes on, quick wash, and heading for London. Then onto the London underground to Baker Street. Then an hour long, trip to Harrow. Followed by a short bus trip, enter stables, find horse, administer healing, horse shows no immediate signs of anything happening, come back home after a long and arduous trip.
One week later, revisit stables. Horse is now fine. His eye condition was now much better. His appearance was also much better. The owner accepts that the horse is much better. I become a very famous man and life is fantastic WRONG!
"It's not the healing, it's the grass he had eaten!" the owner had told Ron. Ron telephoned me to tell me what the owner had said. I was crest fallen. "Eating bloody grass? The miserable old ******". I was so pi**ed off, I told Ron I would call him later. No fortune to be made. Not even a drink for my time or a kiss my a***, sweet FA. I sat and spoke to John my guide thoroughly disconsolate. What an ungrateful cow I thought! I picked up my pen and paper and began to write, "Now Gary" said John, "What was the purpose of you giving that healing to the horse? Was it so you could become rich and famous may I ask? Or was it to help that poor horse? Now you see Gary that is a lesson in humanity." After some deep reflection I realised

that the selfish I am had been humbled. Point taken John boy! The big I am certainly needed some refinement. I knew this but how did I achieve it? When would I achieve it? Would I ever achieve it? What a hard lesson that was! I needed a break from it all so I telephoned Margaret. She picked up my feelings of depression and invited me over. I could hardly wait. I desperately needed new conversation and to clear my head. "Come over today if you are doing nothing better?" "Thank you, I will." I caught the next train out and arrived some three hours later. I opened the patio doors and from the balcony looked out across a beautiful manmade lake to see the sun dancing on the water below. It was just then that a thought popped into mind, write a book and call it 'In Search of the Swan.' The term 'swan' had appeared once before in a letter from Deborah M to me some months back. Could that message be connected to the book I am to write? I wondered. I liked the title but write a book? An horrendous thought for someone whose grammar was zilch. Betting slips, no problem, and a book? Forget it! A book about what exactly? A swan? Don't make me laugh! Book begins. A swan is white, beautiful and apparently mates for life, that's two lines, book finished. Write a book? Dream on! They do say that everyone has a book in them but that seemed a totally unrealistic proposition. After a weekend at Margaret's I felt great. Much refreshed and quite happy within myself. Margaret on hearing the story of the horse healing wondered if I could help her daughter Nicole who had suffered from Rheumatoid Arthritis since birth. Next time I am over I will meet her and we shall see if the healing can help.

I thanked Margaret for her hospitality and went home pondering the ludicrous suggestion of me writing a book. In search of the swan um, lovely title though!

# CHAPTER FIVE

## *A PORTRAIT OF SPIRIT*

Around the April of 1996 I took a trip back into Basildon town centre to see Marion the Tarot reader at the hairdressers, she looked great. We talked about events that had happened since the last time I saw her and we had much to talk about, when in walked a young man. He was no more than nineteen. Tall, athletic build with glasses, but it wasn't his looks that struck me, but this foreboding sense of emptiness with him. I had never experienced this feeling before but looking at him he appeared an empty shell. He asked if he could have a reading from Marion and immediately she said "No, I am sorry love you are too young."
I wasn't surprised she told him that, because I knew she had felt the same as me. He told her he was an artist and that he was at college, but she wouldn't budge on the reading and told him to go home and paint her a picture of spirit. "Spirit? What is that?" he asked. "Go home and paint me anything then" she replied. He left and Marion looked at me with a sense of did you pick that up? She also felt a kind of emptiness with him. "I don't feel he has long for this world Marion." "No, neither do I" she replied. It was a rather strange thing to say about someone so young. The very next day the boy returned but Marion was not there, so the boy left a painting he had done at the request of Marion with the other girls at the hairdressers. He had painted his self-portrait. Some three months later I got a telephone call from Marion and she said. "Do you remember that young lad who came into my office that day,

the one we had a bad feeling about?" "Yes" "Well, yesterday a lady came in for a reading. She sat next to me and I read her cards. I picked up the loss of a son and with that I went and got that portrait the boy had left me. The lady was astounded because the portrait when I showed her turned out to be her son, who had taken his own life by throwing himself under a train some three weeks before. She never knew he had been to Marion and she also said he never did portraits. How remarkable then that his attempt at painting 'spirit' that Marion had asked him to do, turned out to be a message or sign for his mother. It was unbelievable. That sense of foreboding I haven't had since but his death came as no surprise to Marion or me. Marion and I kept in touch until our paths went there separate ways. Marion had taken me that little bit further down the road; another catalyst whose role in my life seemed minor at the time of meeting her but would again prove to be significant. Just a few years back I wasn't totally convinced in the world of the so called 'paranormal' and now I lived and breathed it. I was beginning to experience remarkable things on a daily basis. Healing with the hands, channelled writings, seeing the future, having visions, truly amazing stuff! I often wonder about some of those poor souls who are classed as schizophrenic, perhaps they too are just like me just what they call psychic or gifted. Perhaps in some cases they just needed to harness those thoughts? Boy, it's a fine line I can tell you. The gambling was more likely to lead to mental health problems than the gift. Some have the idea that to have the gifts you need to be fully trained, pious etc but I never had any training whatsoever and no one could say I was pious! I was always swearing like a trooper at the horses that disguised themselves as donkeys amongst thoroughbreds during the races. Well at least that is how it looked to me! Even though I was going through some depressing gambling times again and a condition called empty wallet, I began to get greater clarity with the channelling. During one writing session I was told my mind would cease to ramble with loads of thoughts. This happened shortly thereafter when I woke up one morning to discover I had no thoughts at all in my head. There were no more rambling thoughts. My mind was completely blank. I used to have all kinds of thoughts whizzing around my head but now there was just emptiness, a void. It was a state of bliss. People have told me it is like that when you meditate, so basically I was in a meditative state all the time. It is rather wonderful. This explained how I was able to hear the dictated words so clearly. This was most beneficial because at times I would channel hundreds of words and the clearer I could hear the words the easier I found it all. Imagine being on a Dictaphone with your boss dictating hundreds of words to you down the earpiece, well this is a similar scenario. It takes incredible powers of concentration. I remember one day writing for over ten minutes solid with no pause or punctuation just a constant stream of words. I have also channelled a Biblical type book, a piece of Latin and a Shakespearian style play too. Not sure of the merits of any of them but they are totally different from my thoughts or style of writing. I began to hear names and places when I gave readings for people and people would often be astounded by what would come through. Many times proof was given to people of a loved one or people they knew who had passed away. Many times information was given to me to pass on I could not possibly have known and many times there were correctly predicted future events that happened. You just never knew with those spirit voices giving you information what you would get. I often couldn't believe it myself. It was mind-boggling at times. I often wondered why I had been given this gift in the first place. I wasn't an angel, far from it. I regret parts of my life and any minor wrong-doing I may have done. But it seems being a goody two shoes isn't a necessary criteria. So it could happen to anyone just like it did me. What it did do is to put me on a good road and that is the road I have travelled ever since, as good a road as I could possibly make it! Life is all about learning and we have all made mistakes. I can understand how people do wrong things when driven by gambling, drugs, and alcohol etc because it can be so destructive. You don't think or act the same when you have a problem of some kind.

All rationality goes out of the window I am afraid. At least with my gift I was able to change my life and my perception of things, which I am so grateful for. Others sometime never see any light in their lives and end up another statistic along life's road. I guess life is about learning and that is part of this magical existence we all have to go through. Various attributes good, bad and indifferent are required to make us what we are as human beings. What is the meaning of life? Who knows?

But sometimes it's good to take stock of what you are truly blessed with. At Ronald's one day we discussed many things about life and I liked to hear his stories about the war. He had stacks of stories to tell and was a fascinating man to talk to. During our conversation I remarked, "Who is Alouicious Ron?"

"Blimey" he said, "That was my nickname in the RAF… how the bloody hell did you get that name?" "Don't ask me!" We laughed so much. He had a wicked sense of humour. We talked about people's reaction to my gifts and he would often talk about Winston Churchill. One story I loved which he told me was when Churchill and his aide were walking through an Art gallery and Churchill remarked "That is a beautiful painting" to which his aide replied "I don't know what you see in that old boy," Churchill retorted "Ah, but don't you wish you could!" That to me epitomizes life. We talked about healing and how that worked. He would often press me for an answer of how it worked but I would always say "Search me Ron. I haven't a clue. All I know is it does". How does it work exactly? No one truly knows. We can all surmise. Some even may believe they truly know, but do they? What I do is place my hands on or near the person or animal, allow my hands to be guided to wherever I feel drawn too and away I go. Something definitely happens and it defiantly works. It has been proven to work not just by me but also throughout history. I cannot explain why you can have two identical cases and one will receive great benefit whilst the other one will have a very limited benefit, it must be something to do with the make up of the individual or animal. Hard to explain that! But as with all aspects of the gift/s it is not an exact science and therefore cannot be truly measured. I am sure it is an energy that we are given through our body that is dissipated through our hands but that is my opinion. When I give healing it normally takes roughly five minutes, if that. It comes from the same source as the channelling I believe but more than that is supposition. I told Ron of Margaret and how she had asked me to help her daughter, which I did with amazing results. Within three months of my helping her with the aid of the spirit guides (inner voices) like John, Nicole had an almost complete recovery from a very debilitating and crippling illness. Her neck was fused at one point and through the healing it freed itself. The healing helped her so much that Margaret wrote to a national newspaper journalist on my behalf she was so pleased with the results. Ron and I discussed the term often used by scientists when discussing 'alternative healing' the term known as 'the placebo effect' but there is no placebo effect where animal healing is concerned. There never has been or ever will be. So that cannot possibly be the answer. In some cases of course it is a placebo effect but certainly not all. To some people it is referred to as 'alternative' but the reality is modern medicine is the 'alternative' because healing with hands has been with us since the beginning of time. Healing is very interesting as a subject matter but some Doctors won't have it that it works. Many are totally opposed to even the thought it may work. Perhaps the fact they need to spend years getting qualified and healers don't as something to do with it? In fairness there are many Doctors beginning now throughout the world who are willing to accept healing and rightly so in my opinion. Besides, modern medicine and drugs are more often than not a cause of problems rather than a cure. From my perspective both are valid in their own way. Ron was simply baffled by it all and he would voice this on every visit I made. One case that certainly baffled us all was when he once asked me to visit his half brother's son in St Mary's Hospital in London. This was to prove one of my most amazing experiences. I found out that his son had aids and that he was in there to die. Ronald's half brother expected no more of me than to give some healing comfort but as God is my witness we got so much more. On first seeing him lying in the bed a weak, frail figure, I swear almost grey in colour I offered him my hand. Shortly thereafter he said he felt something happen to him like some sort of energy go through him. Five minutes later he left his hospital bed and walked unaided to the lift. We offered to help him but he refused and said he was ok. He went with us to the canteen, had a cup of tea and returned to his room. His father told me in private his son had not left his bed for at least three days and was taking fluids, so he was astonished by what he had witnessed, us too! That was the last I saw of him but I was told he was still alive two years later. How true that is I have no idea but I would like to think it was true, I am sure it was. Little did Ronald know one day I would help him with healing. It was on one such visit to Ronald that he found healing would help him. We sat after eating breakfast of which Ron had made me a porridge (which the prison would have been proud of). I actually thought it was plaster, but Ronald was not amused by my jest. Anyway after his little tantrum we sat and discussed Shakespeare and were in the throes of great debate about the man when Ronald complained he could not get out of the chair, to which I remarked "You always have your ar** stuck in the chair!" but my laughter turned to horror as I realised he was in trouble. He asked me to pull him up out of the chair which I did, when suddenly he collapsed. He told me he had lost all the dexterity in his hands and legs. I was horrified. He begged me to give him healing but I insisted he went to hospital, but he would have none of it. So

we made a compromise I would give him healing and after the healing he would go straight to the hospital or at the very least his own Doctor. “Ok Ron, but I can’t promise you anything. If they can help you I am sure they will”. With great trepidation I placed my hands on the right hand side of his head and within seconds he told me he felt pins and needles throughout his body, these were then replaced by a great warmth. 10 minutes of healing (more than usual) and his body began to return to normal. I was thrilled to have my dear friend back as was, but I still wanted him to get a check up. His neighbours kindly took him to his doctor who examined him not knowing of my healing and said Ronald was absolutely fine and all he could put Ronald’s problem down to was stress. Stress my ar**! I don’t ever remember Ron getting stressed in the 2 1/2 years I knew him. Anyway the next morning as John my guide had promised Ronald would be his old self and he was, in fact he drove me home to Essex where I then lived and that was a seventy-mile round trip. He drove like a bloody lunatic. He scared the hell out of me. Sterling Moss had nothing on him. I don’t think the healing had given him carte blanche to feel immortal!
The angels were definitely singing in my ear that day I can tell you. In his letter of thanks Ronald describes the healing as ‘a miracle I would not have believed it possible’ me neither!

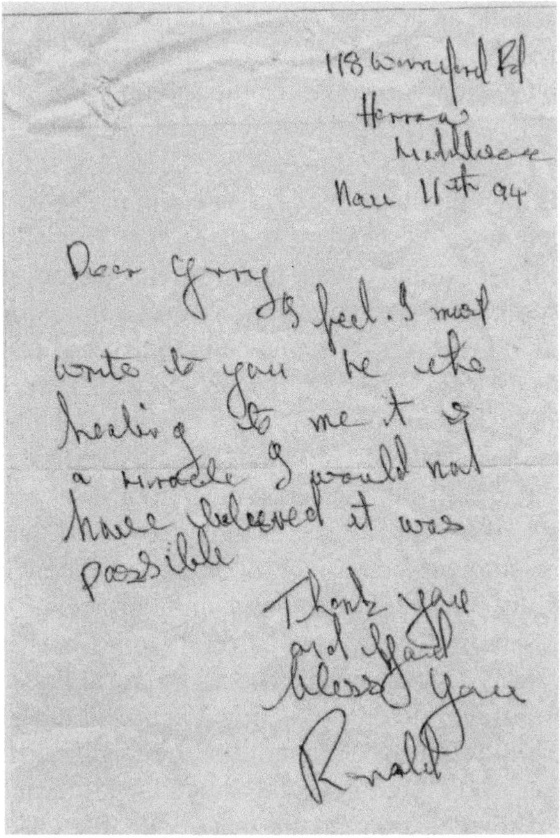
118 [illegible] Rd
Harrow
Middlesex
Nov 11th 94

Dear Gerry
Its feel. I must write to you re the healing. To me it is a miracle I would not have believed it was possible

Thank you and God bless you
Ronald

*A letter of thanks from Ronald Bailey*

Despite the shock of that incident Ronald was certainly back to his old self and two weeks later I was at his home again and did some psychic work with him. Through the words of my spirit guide I had assured him he was in rude health and he did say he certainly felt that way. During this particular session I predicted he would meet a younger female. I said, "Ron you have a young bird coming into your life. She is about half your age, you lucky bastard!" Ron laughed at the thought of a 76 year

old wining and dining a young dolly. Never mind the rest of it. "You are fine now after your little turn, I reckon you could handle a young bird" I said. I will never forget the look on his face that day. Nor will I forget the look on his face the next time I saw him 3 months later, when he told me he had indeed met a woman half his age. They had been getting closer and closer, and now was the time to consummate the relationship. Only one problem his manhood was limper than a balloon that had just been deflated. Never mind, Ron had the answer. There it stood on the table top as I entered the front room. A bottle of do it yourself 'erect a decent manhood' injector kit. Guaranteed to please!
I laughed my head off as Ronald explained that he had tried the injector only the previous week and it certainly worked. There was a slight problem.
It caused his penis to stay hard for well over two hours. My face dropped as he asked me to inject him with the stuff just this time to prevent the two-hour extravaganza. "Enough for about half hour will do," he said. "I put in far too much the last time!"
"Ronald, I don't think I am that good a friend"
I told him. Even a dear friend such as I have a line that should never be crossed and Ronald wanted me to cross it. The thought of clasping his fruit and two veg in my hand whilst administering the wonder fluid with the other, did not feel with me great anticipation I can tell you. Ronald went on to explain his erection problem took place whilst he was shopping in Waitrose 'the up market' supermarket. I was in hysterics at the thought of his manhood resembling Cleopatra's needle and remaining solid for over two bloody hours.
I envisaged him pushing the trolley round the isles with no hands! Oh my God come to think of it how

horrendous is that? Thank God they didn't have self service then! The young lady had certainly made Ronald feel twenty one again. He told me he had bought weights to build his muscles, a bike for ultimate fitness and started jogging to achieve an Adonis body. What a bloody fool! A telephone call came two days after Christmas having previously spoken to Ronald on Christmas Eve from a mutual friend of mine and Ronald's named Russell. "Ron is dead!" he said. "He died of a heart attack on boxing day." I was totally gutted; not only had I lost my best friend but he had died a most ignominious death in the street, on my birthday of all days, Boxing Day. It was like losing my right arm. I often wonder what killed him. Was it sex with a younger woman? The now famed penis injector? (He missed out on Viagra by months) or my friends from the other world just saying Ronald your time is up, time to say goodbye to Gary and goodbye to life. I know wherever he is now he will be reading this book and laughing his boll***ks off. I loved that old bastard, I truly did. True friends in a lifetime can be counted on one hand. If you can count more than two fingers you have been truly blessed.

# CHAPTER SIX

## *THE DEATH OF ONESELF*

After Ronald's shock death it took me sometime to adjust to life without him. Who would listen to my every word now? He was like my right arm and now he was no longer there. Waking up the morning after being told was the worst, that realisation your best friend is no longer there. Picking up the phone to hear those words "204-0574 Gary dear boy" down the telephone would no longer happen. The fact I met him through John's words telling me to go to Belgrave square, made Ron very special to me. For him to die on my birthday also meant his memory would stay with me forever. Ronald dying in the street pains me somewhat, because he was such a proud man, and that ignominious death did not befit his life. But I know that a beautiful soul left his prostrate body that day to venture to pastures new. "What now, John?" I asked. Now there would be new depths of despair to conquer? But with this would also come a chance to re-evaluate myself. Perhaps Ronald's death would be a blessing in disguise and help me to achieve a breakthrough of the old self. Shortly after Ronald's cremation attended by actress and long time friend Sheila Hancock, he had his ashes gloriously scattered across his little piece of heaven called Bournemouth, just as he wished. I took stock of my life and like a snake shedding his skin I could feel the inner me breaking through. A change was imminent and it needed to be. The day after Ron's death I can remember writing and got a rather poignant message through, it read "You know life is eternal don't you Gary, that is how you are able to communicate with us. We have passed but have lived as you and Ron before. Shed no tears for Ron embrace his passing as a new beginning. Remember Gary, all roads lead to France." "Why do all roads lead to France John?" "Time will tell Gary, time will tell." Now I was ready to accept that John and co were truly speaking from beyond the grave. Seeing Ulla proved to me that ghosts existed. Now I was ready to accept that on death we do not die, but move on to another form of existence.

Months before Ronald's passing I sat watching a television programme on the BBC about the paranormal called 'Out of this World'. I thought it would be a good idea to put myself forward and challenge the conventional view that television seems to portray, that paranormal gifts haven't been proved as yet. I felt it would be a great opportunity for me to demonstrate my ability and for the programme to find an answer to my apparent gifts. Having listened to many scientists who appeared on various television programmes telling everyone that more research was needed, I wondered just how much research was in fact needed. After all things relating to the paranormal had been documented since year dot and many hugely intelligent men have and had written on the subject convinced of paranormal phenomena. Many worldwide have certainly believed in the paranormal and spirit communication. Many of those people considered today as some of the greatest writers, greatest philosophers, greatest artists, greatest poets and indeed minds of all time. There are substantial eyewitness accounts and written accounts centuries old. Royalty and many world leaders have used and still use psychics and yet these scientists appearing on these types of programmes continued to say that there was no evidence to back the claims psychic and paranormal phenomena existed. I was amazed as many genuine people were ridiculed as being deluded. I thought at the time the anti-psychic brigade were talking complete nonsense and through my development I knew they were talking nonsense. To me paranormal phenomena did exist for certain. It was during one such programme that I observed the resident scientist who seemed to have an answer to everything put to him. They didn't however put forward a case against channelling like mine or in fact a case for it, they just never included it. How odd I thought. The Scientist was given things that I felt were all too easy to debunk and ridicule, which I found somewhat demeaned a probably well-intentioned programme. I found no joy in my attempts to appear on the programme. All letters sent seemed doomed to failure. Was it the way I had constructed the letters? Did my explanation of the ability I had sound too far fetched? Would my ability have been unexplainable to the resident Scientist leaving him with no answer perhaps? I felt for one that I described it well and how it actually was in my letters but no one appeared interested. I found this difficult to understand and a bit disheartening. Surely if people wanted to find the truth regarding the paranormal, well mine was an interesting case in point. I thought I would take the opportunity to contact the Society for Psychical Research after someone suggested they were the people to contact. They sent along a scientist to see me called Dr Foster. What a waste of time that was. He spent over two hours with me. I believe no amount of evidence would have been

good enough for him and I was right. Had God appeared before him he would have dismissed it! I quickly realised this was one road to forget about. I would strongly advise anyone against this route as it doesn't seem genuine to me. I didn't at the time and still don't believe they have any intention of finding the truth but that is just my opinion.
The resident scientist on 'Out of this World' was a certain Dr Richard Wiseman. The address given was Hertfordshire University. I thought it would be a good idea to contact him direct as I couldn't get any joy with the show or the society. I wrote to him explaining my writing ability and received his reply some days later. He sent me a task to complete. Fill the boxes with symbols it read. The more symbols you get right (the answers were already with Wiseman and co) the more possibility there was that it is not by chance you got them right, and therefore there maybe some form of E.S.P happening. Only one problem you had to rely on their honesty that you got the answers right. You could have got them all right and might never have known! It all sounded a bit dodgy to me. One question going through my mind at this point was what the hell had putting symbols in boxes got to do with a channelling ability? Answer: Absolutely nothing! This test seemed ridiculous and I never gave it much credence, at least not when it came to explaining what I did. I wrote back to Dr Wiseman and asked him about my writings. How were they derived? Where he thought the content came from? How he thought the future was predicted through the writing? How hundreds of words could be written without pause in conversational text, with

no punctuation and yet the work made perfect sense? Never mind the quality of the content or the style and personality throughout the different works. He mentioned nothing of my questions in his second reply and said I could not be tested if I didn't complete the ridiculous test as this was testing policy? I thought if that's how they test for a paranormal ability no wonder they appear never to prove anything in the so-called scientific community. I thought my abilities although illogical were at least self-explanatory. At least the gifts could be seen by eye and they were tangible. As for understanding? Well, that's another matter and that is for the Scientists and investigations to conclude. Why the reluctance to investigate me? My ability is one which definitely provokes the most profound thought. Why some intelligent people fail to see it amazes me! Perhaps they just don't wish to see it? Perhaps they find it intimidating or even frightening? Perhaps it puts into doubt Science and Religion and all they have learned? Questions need answers and I wasn't getting any. I found one answer on reading a magazine about the paranormal called 'Encounters'. I was astonished to discover an article of the said Dr Wiseman. It somewhat confirmed my suspicion. He is reported to have said and I quote 'If psychic powers exist at all-and it's a big if-then it's a small ability which you wouldn't notice in everyday life.' I found that an amazing statement from an 'open minded' scientist. The more I investigated the TV sceptics, scientists and parapsychologists the more the question was raised of why television used people who were obviously not open minded at all but very close minded, and with seemingly no interest in finding the truth as regards paranormal matters.

I was even more amazed as I read further his article in the 'Encounters' magazine when Dr Wiseman adds when asked the question if any psychic had convinced him of any ability? His answer was an emphatic "No"... this was followed by the same old anti-psychic nonsense ending with and I quote "I'm very much convinced that if there are psychic powers and its a big if... they are not large and they are not the sort of things people can produce a demonstration of and you go 'oh wow, that's absolutely incredible." I felt that was a preposterous statement but then understood a little more clearly when I realised Dr Wiseman had sat on the so called 'investigation' committee for the Society of Psychical Research. My previous experience of this organisation had left a lot to be desired and their research simply had to be questioned. I gave up on scientific explanation from that moment. Others I had met had experienced similar dismissive treatment of their abilities, so I thought there is no point going down a closed road. Others like him for example Dr Chris French etc are in my opinion paid debunkers who will never find the answer. My view was this, I knew what I had existed. I knew I need not prove the origin of the extraneous source for that was for others to do. I would like to think that anything which is not considered explained by natural law is investigated thoroughly to eliminate all possibilities. I in fact wrote to James Randi another well-known debunker of psychics in 1994 and he sent me a postcard back, which ridiculed what I had said. Randi offered a million dollars to anyone who can prove they have any kind of psychic or paranormal ability. But before all you talented psychics rush out to collect the money, be warned! You have more chance of a double lottery win. His contract has more ‘get outs’ than Houdini. No one ever has or ever will collect the money. My advice is don’t even go there! Randi had no interest in investigating my claims further which says it all!

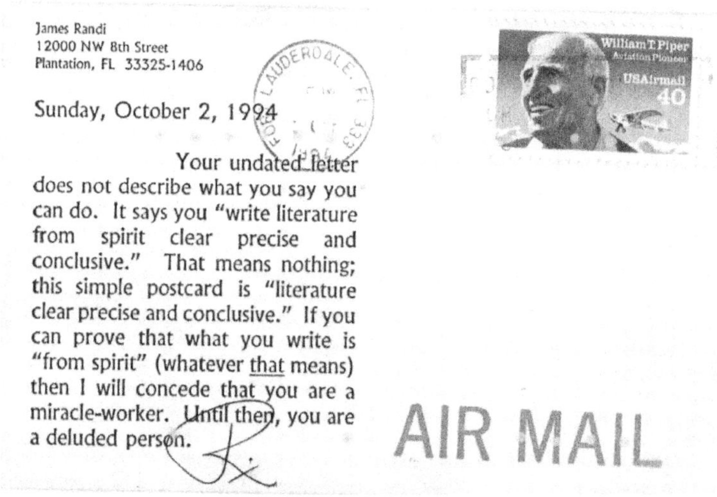
James Randi
12000 NW 8th Street
Plantation, FL 33325-1406

Sunday, October 2, 1994

Your undated letter does not describe what you say you can do. It says you "write literature from spirit clear precise and conclusive." That means nothing; this simple postcard is "literature clear precise and conclusive." If you can prove that what you write is "from spirit" (whatever that means) then I will concede that you are a miracle-worker. Until then, you are a deluded person.

AIR MAIL

*Postcard from Randi*

I did some research on the researchers of the paranormal, people like Dr Wiseman, James Randi, Dr Susan Blackmore (now interestingly a Zen Buddist I believe), Dr Chris French and others and discovered they all have one common denominator. They are all set in stone sceptics. So how they can appear on radio and TV giving a so-called unbiased opinion is beyond me. You cannot be unbiased when you believe ‘it doesn’t exist!’ as you have already decided that it doesn’t. What I don’t quite understand is that if it doesn’t exist as they claim what the hell do they research and investigate? What is the point? I found a couple more articles of Dr Wiseman's that surprised me somewhat, one from a BBC newsonline article entitled 'A Wiseman debunks psychics' where he was quoted as saying `but, at the end of the day he (Wiseman) recognises that he will never be able to persuade the true believers psychics Do Not Exist. All he wants is to encourage a little common sense. There, a nice open-minded statement. I then found another article from Encounters magazine, which really had me rolling about in fits of laughter when Dr Wiseman was asked the question "What do you recommend if people want to test psychic claims? "We're pushing people to consult with magicians or security experts as the appropriate source of expertise." If that wasn't bad enough I uncovered a book written by Dr Wiseman and Robert Morris called 'Guidelines to Testing Psychic Claimants'. On page 21 it is written `after a few meetings with the claimant, researchers have to decide whether they wish to embark on an investigation. Researchers may consider such work unfeasible or undesirable. A claimant may not be able to formulate a claim that can be easily tested. This sounds to me like an excellent get out clause thus eliminating those from testing that they cannot explain. I also found on page 27 it is written 'potential claimants could also be informed that research policy dictates that ALL reports of an investigation will NOT include the name of the claimant, unless (perhaps) the claimant has been shown to be fraudulent.' So in other words if you were genuine no one would ever know! But they are more than happy to expose the fake or fraud. Then we have the sentiments of another well known television 'open-minded' Dr Chris French often

French “French is under no illusions as to the prejudices of many of his colleagues.” Most psychologists could reasonably be described as uninformed skeptics – a minority could reasonably be described as prejudiced bigots - where the paranormal is concerned". (The Skeptic 14(9)) He is also more self-aware than most skeptics about his own prejudices. As he wrote in The Skeptic, 14(4): “I am biased in my approach to evidence relating to the paranormal…..I make no claim to be a neutral assessor of the evidence”. Something wrong there don’t you think? I felt these kinds of scientists had no interest in serious paranormal research and that it was a complete waste of time and public money quite frankly. The truth should be the only consideration. If they were serious about research then people like me must be researched. If after serious research it was found to be true then what I claim should be made public knowledge. As already said the gifts are not an exact science and should be treated as such. I did once briefly meet Dr Peter Fenwick a consultant Neuro-Psychiatrist who is very interested in the field of NDE (near death experience) and a letter I got from him implied he never doubted my ability. Perhaps I should have seen if he or his colleagues would have done more investigative work rather than the silly Wiseman/French and Randi route, which in my humble opinion and I now realise has no scientific respectability. My former friend Margaret couldn't believe the way people avoided me like the plague when it came to researching what I had. Margaret had a few friends that one would consider intelligent and with a decent amount of brain matter and those that I met certainly had no rational answer to what had been demonstrated to them by me. So it then raised the question of how come these high-minded individuals realised the magnitude of the ability and others like Dr Wiseman, Mr Randi and certain members of the society for psychical research did not. I did wonder if there is not an underlying reason behind their miserable attempts to find the truth where psychic and paranormal things were concerned. If you want science or any organizations to look into your abilities make sure they are open minded and really have the determination to uncover the truth. In fact Dr Wiseman appeared in an experiment called 'The Scole experiment' some years back. A mammoth series of exhaustive tests and the results are well worth a read. How much of it is worthy of the name 'truth' is another matter, but some of it is interesting. There is also a paper by Paul Bernstein PhD on the scientific research into intuition (sixth sense) and its conclusion proves beyond all doubt that after extensive research it has been scientifically proven. In fact the so called 'father of modern science' Einstein, made the following statement "The intuitive mind is a sacred gift and the rational mind is a faithful servant. We have created a society that honours the servant and has forgotten the gift." – Einstein, which leaves little doubt he believed in its existence too! When the sceptics say there is no evidence I am afraid they are going against science itself! Margaret was of the same opinion of these so called experts; she even introduced me to one individual, a highly respected former top C.I.D Officer. His wife ended up being the catalyst for a series of meetings, which started with a Surrey psychic, two trips to Malvern Hills one of which was a party. At the party I was given an introduction to an American lady named

Rachelle. She decided that her and her husband would take me back to Bray in Hertfordshire, miles from where I lived. For some unexplained reason I thought it was a good idea! I was then introduced to her friend and it all seemed rather surreal. As just two weeks later whilst at this friend's flat, news filtered through that Princess Diana had died in a Paris car crash around six weeks after I had written to her, an inspired letter and sent her one of my poems. Ironically the poem was called 'a painting of life' (featured in this book). I felt it was the right thing to do to contact her as I felt she needed some 'inspired' words. I hope my message helped her in some small way. I began to think my letters to people had a curse attached to them when I later wrote to Matthew Harding (a then director at Chelsea FC). He was killed in a helicopter crash after returning from a midweek match in Bolton. Once again this was only weeks after receiving one of my letters. I don't suppose anyone wants a letter from me now do they? Anyway back to the story. I was asked whilst in Bray if I could give a reading to a friend of Rachelle the American lady. It turned out this lady was French. Straight away the thought entered my head of the message I had been given by John and co months before that 'all roads lead to France'. "Sounds fine to me!" I said. I felt good about this. I can always feel if a person is right to read (give insight to) and this felt right and that was when I met Isabelle. She was an attractive 30 something but more importantly French. Could this have been the clue of the 'all roads lead to France' message I kept receiving? We arranged to meet again and I quickly realised that Isabelle was part of my path. Three months later we had developed a good understanding of one another and she invited

me over to France. She lived in Le Mans home of the 24 hr road race. After an arduous journey we arrived. Isabelle informed me that healing was thoroughly accepted in Le Mans and it was commonplace. So if I wanted to give anyone healing or a reading for that matter it would be ok to do so. This made a change from England with its sceptical eye cast upon people like me. Whilst there, we visited her close friend Bridget. Bridget had said she was very interested in English culture and my conversation on Shakespeare although limited, interested her. I have a book she said it maybe of some value to you? I picked up the book and it was called 'Foucault's Pendulum' by Umberto Eco.
"I will purchase a copy of this when in England, but thanks for offering to lend it to me." Although I had limited French I could see references in the book to Dee, Shakespeare, someone called Francis Bacon and the Knights Templar. It was all fascinating stuff from what I could make out. "On second thoughts Bridget would you mind if I do take the book home? "I can get Isabelle to translate it on the ferry home." "No problem" she said. After coffee we made tracks and found a beautiful shop that sold books, crystals etc on our way to Le Mans town centre. I found loads of books on the Knights Templar alongside the Cathars which the French people had talked about and the English Freemasons. I had no idea of why these books were sectioned together but jotted down a few titles.
We had a great week and I felt there was something very special about France. On the ferry home Isabelle kindly read me sections of the book which were somewhat heavy going as her heart wasn't in it. Being Shakespeare and Dee were mentioned in the book, I felt it would be advisable to do some

serious research when I got back home to England. There was just so much I didn't understand.
Why was I being guided to historical figures like Shakespeare and Dee? All I knew about them at this point was that Shakespeare had written some plays and sonnets and was apparently called 'The Sweet Swan of Avon' which I found interesting from the point of view it gave reference to the swan and that Dee was an Alchemist come Astrologer for Elizabeth the 1st and who like me had conversations with spirits. The Dee, Shakespeare link would indeed prove to be something very special. Tired I asked Isabelle to read no more and my head hit the pillow in contemplation and excitement of just what the book might reveal.
The following morning we arrived safely back on these shores and although a little fatigued from the journey I couldn't wait to get stuck into some research and made some enquiries as regards the home of John Dee. I was aware from my previous research he had lived in Mortlake, Surrey and a friend suggested that I try the old town hall in Richmond to see if they had any relevant information on him. From a telephone call to them I found that Richmond old town hall possessed plenty of information on Dr Dee. I visited there at the first opportunity and found the place I needed to be was in the local studies room. I asked one of the staff for anything they had on Dee and was surprised when the lady came back with a box full. Within the box my eyes feasted upon relevant facts on Dee's life and one letter in particular excited me, it was a letter written by a Dr William Montgomerie. The title Dr Dee to Mr Shakespeare! This was the first time any relevant connection had been made between Dee and Shakespeare in my research. The

letter was written in the eighties and was written in a rather strange way in the form of a coded message. I photocopied as much material as I possibly could on Dee and felt like a kid in the proverbial sweet shop. I tried to contact Mr Montgomerie the author of the letter with regard to the content of the very strange message but had no luck. Had he long moved? Had he died? Who knows? I still don't know many years later. Perhaps someone out there could enlighten me as I would love to know? I took the material home and began studying. Dee was as already pointed out Queen Elizabeth the 1st's Astrologer. He was also an Alchemist, an Occultist, Mathematician and a Spy. A man versed in the classics. A rather brilliant man. Dee was a man of the very highest intellect.
A man who had studied Latin, Greek and Hebrew. Biblical study, the kabala and was much travelled. Most importantly for me he was a man who said he thanked the 'spirit who writes these things rapidly through me; I hope and I believe I am merely the quill, which traces these characters.' This quotation referring to his book the Monas Hieroglyphica 1564 in which he said he channelled its contents in twelve days. My goodness I thought Dee amazingly like me was channelling from the spirit world. This for me was a great discovery to find someone with a similar gift. Shakespeare on the other hand I found to be a complete enigma. Having flicked through the book Geraldine sent me 'the Shakespeare conspiracy' I couldn't believe how many things just didn't add up. His life was shrouded in mystery. Apart from the letter Dr Dee to Mr Shakespeare which obviously was a modern writing, nothing appeared to connect the two directly from an historical standpoint, which I found strange being as

both Shakespeare and Dee were seemingly heavily into the mystical side of things. Both were around at the same period of history and both had connections to the same people. And although that letter wasn't historical evidence linking the two its contents were very mysterious. I researched Shakespeare and his life and was truly amazed by the lack of information that was historical and fact. There was plenty of myth though. A few questions I pondered were these; Where did Shakespeare obtain his enormous wealth of knowledge? Why was there is no record of high academic education? It appeared Shakespeare wrote about an enormity of subjects wide and diverse. Well over thirty different subjects in fact, all with an in-depth knowledge. Although a high education would not make him a writer, it would help to perhaps explain his expansive knowledge to some degree? Was he self-taught I wondered? Why were there no original paintings of him? All paintings and prints are mere supposition. He never left any manuscripts or documents, books or letters. Nothing left in his will that gave indication he was a writer, no mentioning of documents, books, letters, manuscripts etc that seemed extraordinary to me for such a prolific writer. Documentation of some sort survives of all the great writers of that period and yet nothing of Shakespeare. Why was it no one in Stratford upon Avon his hometown appeared to know of his activities as a writer? From all known records no one knew him as a playwright or writer, but merely as a grain merchant, of which his bust gives indication too, in which his hands are placed on a sack (The bust was in those days indicative of your profession). And yet some thirty odd years after his death it was reconstructed to show Shakespeare in a completely different light this time as a writer. With pen in one hand and parchment in the other thus depicting his profession as a writer? The two busts shown in surviving drawings from two books Sir William Dugdale's 'Antiquities of Warwickshire' 1656 and the other in an illustration in Nicolas Rowe's biography of Shakespeare in some account of the life of Mr William Shakespeare from 1709. The more I began to research the more seemingly absurd it became. Just why was the bust changed? Today you pay £1.00 to enter the Trinity Church where Shakespeare is laid to rest, and where the bust can be seen. And yet there is no mention whatsoever of the bust alteration nor is there any mention of it in the literature of the Shakespeare Birthplace trust for some unknown reason. Shakespeare the greatest writer of all time, and yet he is a complete enigma. I even found out that what is supposed to be his actual birthplace is nothing of the sought, despite the entire Birthplace literature indicating it is. The actual site proclaimed as his birthplace wasn't built until Shakespeare was eleven years old. There is not one jot of historical factual evidence to suggest he was born where it is claimed. Worse still, people from all over the world pay to see this site they are told is the birthplace! Shakespeare's birth and death date is apparently the 23rd of April or St George's day this is also seemed very odd. I concentrated so much at times trying to piece my very own jigsaw that I frequently had headaches but something was driving me on to find out more. I had gone from someone not interested in much apart from curry and crumpet, betting slips and bonking to a studious individual, who greedily spent hours to himself. I went from being someone

relatively uneducated and totally uncultured to being someone arguably very well educated.
I developed not only an interest in History but Art, Classical music, Poetry, Philosophy, Politics and of course my love of the mysterious path. Finding out the Shakespeare connection was vital. I had not been taken down this road of Shakespeare for nothing. I was absolutely determined to find out the answers. An understanding was of the utmost importance. My search for the Swan was gathering momentum and would undoubtedly include Dee and Shakespeare. The change in me was staggering, it was as if someone had put the old Gary in a bin and pulled out a new one. A whole new version of Gary. Mind you, I wasn't complaining. It was purposeful, exciting and for the first time in my life I really enjoyed education. My mind was becoming crammed with information. Not only from all the research I done and become encapsulated with, but also my hours of channelling the philosophy, poetry etc. Every last detail of study needed investigating. Just one tiny clue could lead to the understanding of the swan. Just as one clue missed could mean a search which would last forever.

*Shakespeare's 'altered' bust*

*Shakespeare's original bust (Dugdale)*

# CHAPTER SEVEN

## *PIECES OF THE PUZZLE*

During research I began to discover much more than I could ever have envisaged. The book of Umberto Eco's namely 'Foucault's Pendulum' was fascinating. I began to get interested in the Knights Templar; an army of brave warrior monks who it is said protected the Christians on their pilgrimage to the holy land. I read somewhere of a battle in which the Templar's fought with enormous bravery in the battle of Gaza 1243. From legend of this battle it is said that only 36 Knights Templar's survived from well over 300 who set forth. Shakespeare's first folio of 1623 contained exactly 36 plays the exact same number as that of the Templars who had survived that battle. During cross-referencing books the number 36 kept appearing in various books.
I felt the number had to be symbolic. I also found another link to the mystery of the Swan that day when discovering the Templar's had an order called 'The Knights of the Swan'. The swan was now a connection to the Templars as well as Shakespeare. The Shakespeare and the swan mystery were at long last gaining some momentum. And the more I discovered and the more intrigued I became. Something was driving me forward in a quest for understanding. A quest to find something, of which I had no idea what I was supposed to be seeking.
It became so annoying at times, teasing, prompting, invariably frustrating. It made it even harder when you begin to realise that history books are full of truths, half-truths and no truth. And the image of

someone counting 36 knights coming through castle gates after a battle seemed more than a little far-fetched. Mind you I was intrigued that Shakespeare's plays totalled 36 as well. Perhaps I was just putting two and two together and coming up with four or was I? Finding answers was like finding winners, bloody nigh on impossible but just when I thought the trail had gone cold after months of activity someone mentioned to me the kabala, an ancient Hebrew teaching in a talk we were having one afternoon, that reminded me that I had read about how Dr Dee had been very much linked to its teachings. I looked through my now growing collection of books but couldn't find much on the subject. I spoke to Margaret later that week and discovered she had recently purchased a book on the teaching of the kabala. "I couldn't read it Margaret, could I?" "Of course, come over" she replied. Bloody Hell I thought I wish I hadn't, as I found it a most complex, mind numbingly boring subject. Perhaps I just wasn't ready to understand it? To say it didn't exactly set my soul on fire is an understatement. At least that is not until I came across the Kether or the Crown, a part of its teaching. There I came across the animal symbol for the Kether and I couldn't believe my eyes. It was the 'swan'. Finding the swan in the book of the Cabala gave me a fresh impetus. Thus reinforcing my view, that I was actually searching for something, not just wasting my time on a fruitless or futile exercise. The curry and crumpet man had certainly come a long way, a very long way!

My next surprise came when Isabelle went on a trip to Chertsey in Surrey and entered an antiques shop. Isabelle excitedly phoned me to tell me of this she had met whilst there. “Gary you must meet her” she said. “Why?” I asked. “Don't ask me why? I just feel you should meet her.” Later that month we went to Chertsey in a search for her. We arrived mid-day to find the shop closed and a found notice pinned to the door. Unfortunately her husband had sadly passed away. Intuition told me I had to contact her even though it was certainly not the best of times to announce myself. I telephoned the number on the notice and a gentleman answered. I didn't know her name but explained that Isabelle had spoken to her a couple of weeks previous and would like to continue in conversation where they left off, if that would be possible? He said her name was Sandy and that he would pass the message on. I never expected anything to happen and wasn't sure I had done the right thing in contacting her especially at such a sad time for her. I went to the car when I suddenly noticed a second hand book shop just a few doors along from the shop of Sandy. I entered the shop and saw a rather imposing figure standing behind the counter. I kept thinking how much he looked like the depiction of ‘Jesus’ or at least a figure from the days of ancient fable with his greying long hair and beard. We had a brief chat and I mentioned a little about my search and that I am very much interested in healing with the hands. He then turned to a lady behind the counter and said, "What do you think my wife does? “I have absolutely no idea” I replied. “She is a healer,” he said. He admitted he was not on her wavelength and had little understanding of what I was involved with. I started to tell him of my weird experiences and although he understood little, he nevertheless he said he found it all fascinating. I introduced myself to them both and found their names to be Patrick and Valerie. I felt that meeting Patrick would be another key in my search and it certainly was that as I returned some three weeks later and started discussing Dee and Shakespeare etc. I asked if he had any books on either subject or perhaps a book on the Freemasons, Knights Templar or any other relevant subject. At this point my only understanding of the Knights Templar were that they were mentioned in Umberto Eco's book 'Foucault's Pendulum' and certain books of them were stacked alongside Freemasonry books in a shop in Le Mans. I felt that the Freemasons and/or the Templars fitted into the puzzle somewhere and somehow. But I couldn't be sure just how important or indeed unimportant they were in connecting everything together. "I certainly have nothing on the Freemasons or the Knights Templar but you may well find some old Shakespeare stuff" he added. "I will have a look" I said. "Do you have Foucault's Pendulum by Umberto Eco?" It certainly would be great to have an English copy for my research. "Umberto Eco?" "Ah yes, he wrote "In the Name of the Rose" I believe. "Sorry I haven't got it in stock. I will see if I can order it for you." As he run his fingers along the computer keys I felt quite excited as if something important was about to be discovered. "Ah yes, here it is, it will take a week or so. Do you want me to order it for you? "

"Yes, please" I replied. "Where should I look for the Shakespeare books? "There just there in front of you" he said. Slowly I turned each book. They were stacked like a row of soldiers. One by one meticulously lifting each book and observing the cover. What's this then? I thought as I unearthed a very old looking book 'The Bacon- Shakespeare Anatomy' by W.S Melsome M.A., M.D. This looks great I thought. I continued to look through the section of books and found a couple of books on the Elizabethan times. It is possible there could be something in these I thought, so I purchased all three. I asked Patrick if he would kindly keep me in mind should any books on the relevant subjects I had mentioned crop up. "Yes, of course" he said. I picked up my books and left. I never looked at the Melsome book for weeks. I often did that with books. Bought them then opened the cover and put them on the shelf gathering dust until such times as I was inspired to pick them up again. I placed it on the shelf amongst the other 30 or so books I had acquired since the search began and that's where it stayed. I began to obtain a real passion for old books. Meeting Patrick had opened an unexpected door and one of importance that would shortly reveal itself.

On one particular day some weeks later I felt inspired to read it so I took it from the shelf. As I read the preface I found that Melsome seemed to think that Francis Bacon and Shakespeare was one and the same person. What on earth was he on about I thought to myself? This sounds like a right load of old b*****ks (pardon the old East End lingo). William Shakespeare a pseudonym for Francis Bacon? It sounded like complete rubbish to me. I had already discovered that Shakespeare was a complete enigma but could he really have been someone else? I realised Shakespeare, his life and works didn't seem to quite add up but it did seem a bit farfetched that this Shakespeare bloke wasn't Shakespeare at all, but some other bloke named Bacon. One thing I did know was that my life was becoming more than a bit consumed in Shakespeare the man. Was Shakespeare an alias of Francis Bacon? Was that such a ludicrous idea? I hadn't a clue but it did make me wonder if this Shakespeare and his works really were what they appeared to be? I had a relentless pursuit with a mystical force driving me forward to find answers and I knew I would not have been so interested in Shakespeare, unless there was a purpose behind it. I had discovered on this road that I was travelling that there was always a reason for something happening. There was always a reason why I had met someone. Always a reason I had come across a certain book or hit upon a certain piece of inspired thought. Maybe I would find the answer of who Shakespeare was? Of course that is supposing he was anyone else other than what the history books claimed? Was my search for the swan to discover the truth about Shakespeare? Wow that would be really exciting if that was the case, time would tell.

On reading the contents of the Melrose book something really made me sit up and think that there really might be something in all this, It read; Chapter one Bacon, Shakespeare and Ecclesiastes. Ecclesiastes being the selfsame man from the Bible that Frankie the medium had told me about in the pub at Southend a couple of years back, she had told me to read Ecclesiastes. To think that I had uncovered a book which had Ecclesiastes coupled on the same page with Bacon and Shakespeare seemed remarkable. Frankie's message like most of what was happening made little sense at the time but now seemed to be fitting into place. There was a distinct pattern emerging. Was I being told Shakespeare had a leading role in a play so mystical, so magical, the whole world were part of

it and they never even knew? Was the interest I began to have for Shakespeare of some much deeper mystical and spiritual significance?
And what about that man Francis Bacon? I knew Dr Dee was a channel similar to me, so now would I discover Bacon also had some connection with the spiritual or mystical element? More research would have to be done. I remembered that during my friendship with Ronald that the figure 1547 kept repeating itself in my mind. “Ronald does 1547 mean anything to you?” “No” he said. He was right it didn’t mean anything personally to him, but it did mean something. On my return to his house I came across something unusual sitting on his table. “What’s this Ron?” I asked. “Oh, it is a paperweight. Not even sure who the picture is on the front” he said. it read Nicolas Hilliard born 1547. Hilliard I was later to discover painted a certain Francis Bacon at the age of eighteen. An inscription around the top of the oval painting in Latin on the paperweight read *'Si tabula darentur digna animam mallem'* (if the mind could have been depicted it would have been a worthy portrait). How strange that another connection should be found with Bacon in such an obscure way. It just had to be right that my guides (inner voices) inspired messages were leading me not only to Shakespeare, Dr Dee but also now to Bacon.
I would skip through book after book looking and searching for anything that would provide me with my next clue and my next journey. My next understanding could come from a word, a line, or a passage in a book, it was amazing. Why pick me to unravel this puzzle? Why couldn’t they (from the spirit world) have picked some studious boffin to do

this job? Instead of someone who had never bothered at school and someone whose brain capacity stretched to no more than an interest in curry, crumpet and losing my money on donkeys! Perhaps that was the key. I had the empty mind that like a canvas could be filled. I became a slave to study, re-educating my mind and at the same time unleashing a monster, that being a quest for mystical knowledge.

I took a journey to Glastonbury after reading Dr Dee had said it to be a truly magical place. Glastonbury I read was considered by Dee as the most sacred place on the earth. I had always wanted to go there and when I got the chance I took it. I really liked it on my first visit I felt it did have something very special about it. Whilst there I visited a place called the Chalice well in all its summer tranquillity and bliss. I spent some time at the well in reflective mood before moving to a local bookshop. The back street bookshop brought my mind much relief from the packed streets outside. I asked the assistant if she had any books on Dee, Bacon or Shakespeare? spotting a book on Dr John Dee as she pointed above my head. It was called 'An explanation on the 'Hieroglyphic Monad' priced at £20.00. The cost suddenly dimmed my intention to purchase. She found nothing on Bacon. What about Shakespeare then I asked? "I don't think I have she replied." As I searched through a maze of books I suddenly came across something, a cream coloured book with black edging. What's this then? Who Wrote Shakespeare by John Mitchell. It was another book questioning Shakespeare's authorship. Brilliant, now this looks fascinating! "How much love" I inquired. "Fiver" she replied “done!” I was later to discover there are many books on the Shakespeare authorship question. It raised in mind the question that if there are so many books written on the subject, then there just had to be something in it? Well at least I was hoping there was! In Glastonbury itself everyone talked about the Tor. “You must go there” they said. Now then where is this ‘Tor’ thing everyone goes on about? Having discovered its location, my eyes pointed skywards. “Bloody hell, I can't climb that.” “Oh yes, you can” said one of my friends. That’s part of the fun.” Having reached the summit I was in desperate need of oxygen, with the thought (what the bloody hell did I do that for?) All this just to climb back down! Anyway done it and got the T-shirt. And armed with yet another book! John Mitchell's book certainly opened my eyes considerably and I learned much, which helped me piece the little things together. I felt like a spider weaving its web. Weaving from the outside all the way in. I always believe that you never believe everything you are told or read, it’s always a good grounding. Hopefully it keeps you from running away with yourself on some wild goose chase. Reading Mitchell’s book also brought in new faces into the equation that of Ben Jonson, Christopher Marlowe and other famous playwrights of Shakespeare’s time. All this research was great for keeping the old nags from ruining my day, but during this period I had a dream and would you bloody believe it was about a horse race. In my dream I saw the race in progress and from out of a pack of horses in the race came one a horse named Tedburrow and he went away from the field to win the race at odds of 11/1. I could clearly see the horse’s number 4. Later during the same sleep I

saw the race again and exactly the same thing happened but this time I was looking at my winning ticket as well. I got up the following morning and bought the Sun newspaper. First race at Newcastle was the 2.10pm and there it was, a horse called Tedburrow. The race consisted of eight runners.
It was an outsider at 11-1, I placed twenty pound to win and just as in my dream the race was run in identical fashion with Tedburrow winning coming from out of the pack. I collected £260. I saw the future in my dream without knowing it was running beforehand or anything. I did suggest to friends and family to back it, but sadly my dream didn't fill them with much enthusiasm. And sadly no one but me backed it!

*Are they the dreams of fools and madmen or realities waiting to happen?*

*Picture of Tedburrow courtesy Copyright ©*
*Steve Parrott*

**NEWCASTLE NORTHU**

**2.10 CHIPCHASE STAKES (GROUP 3) (Class A); value to the winner £20,300; 6f (8 runners)**

**1** 980860 **HURRICANE FLOYD 7 (T;D)**
(2) D Nicholls 4-9-2 .................... **K Darley 85**
*Runs: 15 Wins: 1 (GF) Places: 3 £24,475*
Yet to add to maiden win in Aug 2000, inconsistent

**2** 414930 **INDIAN SPARK 11 (C,D)**
(3) J Goldie 8-9-2 .................... **A Culhane 96**
*Runs: 81 Wins: 12 (F, 4GF, 2G, 2GS, 2S, H) Places: 11 £154,690*
Better at 5f, won at this 2-day meeting last June

**3** 45-548 **MISRAAH 7**
(8) Sir M Stoute 5-9-2 .................... **R Hills 96**
*Runs: 17 Wins: 3 (GF, G, GS) Places: 2 £75,407*
5f Listed win, drops down from Gr1, loves fast ground

**4** 87-410 **TEDBURROW 44 (CD,D)**
(4) E Alston 10-9-2 .......... **Dean McKeown●99**
*Runs: 81 Wins: 20 (F, 12GF, 6GS, S) Places: 11 £311,520*
Won this in 2000 but only 2 out of 20 since, best at 6f

**5** 011-27 **VISION OF NIGHT 7 (D)**
(7) J Dunlop 6-9-2 .................... **K Fallon 97**
*Runs: 25 Wins: 8 (4GF, 3G, GS) Places: 6 £181,775*
Gr2 winner, his last 5 wins were all in Aug

**6** 1-0141 **JUST JAMES 10 (D)**
(1) J Noseda 3-8-13 .................... **O Peslier 83**
*Runs: 6 Wins: 3 (GF, G, S) £78,027*
2 last-to-1st wins on fast ground, career best latest

**7** 513-21 **MARIKA 21 (D)**
(6) G Wragg 4-8-13 .................... **D Holland 82**
*Runs: 6 Wins: 2 (GF, S) Places: 2 £26,343*
Won 1m mdn & 6f Listed (both Haydock), tough, in form

**8** 71-393 **ASHDOWN EXPRESS 13 (C)**
(5) C Wall 3-8-9 .................... **T Quinn 84**
*Runs: 9 Wins: 3 (F, GF, GS) Places: 4 £23,219*
3rd both 6f races, wins have come at 7f & 1m

**SUN BETTING:** 5-2 Vision Of Night, 7-2 Misraah, 9-2 Marika, 5 Just James, 10 Tedburrow, Ashdown Express, 12 Indian Spark
**WHERE FAVOURITES FINISHED:** 1 2 1 6 1
**2001: Volata 8-9 T E Durcan 6-4 fav (M Tompkins) drawn 9, 12 ran.**

**SUN FORM**

**HURRICANE FLOYD** (9-0) 20-1 ridden and weakened 2f out, 16th of 28 (btn 11l) to Capricho (8-11) (Ascot 6f hcap (B) £57,816 good to firm).
**INDIAN SPARK** (9-2) 25-1 front rank, gradually weakened, 12th of 15 (btn 4l) to Dominica (8-7) (Ascot 5f Grp 2 (A) £78,300 good).
**VISION OF NIGHT** (9-4) 12-1 ridden 2f out, weakened 1f out, 7th of 12 (btn 6¾l) to Malhub (9-4) **MISRAAH** (9-4) 11-1 soon beaten, 8th (btn 8¾l) (Ascot 6f Grp 1 (A) £144,280 good to firm).
**MISRAAH** (9-1) 6-1 ridden over 2f out, kept on, 5th of 12 (btn 1l) to Invincible Spirit (9-5) **INDIAN SPARK** (9-1) 12-1 no impression, 9th (btn 4¼l) **TEDBURROW** (9-1) 16-1 no impression 1f out, 11th (btn 5¼l) (York 6f Grp 3 (A) £34,800 good to firm).
**JUST JAMES** (8-11) 20-1 kept on to lead close home, bt Steenberg (8-11) nk (15 ran) (Ascot 7f Grp 3 (A) £43,500 good).
**MARIKA** (9-0) 3-1 fav stayed on, all out, bt Palace Affair (9-0) sh hd (9 ran) (Haydock 6f Listed (A) £15,544 soft).
**ASHDOWN EXPRESS** (8-10) 12-1 kept on, 3rd of 7 (btn 2¼l) to Palace Affair (8-12) (Salisbury 6f Listed (A) £14,094 good).

*Original Sun newspaper cutting*

I have given people readings where I have described people who have died and what they had died with, given names, places, predicted the future, given people personal insight, seen miracles performed through healing, channelled with great speed up to and sometimes beyond 70 words per minute, written works far beyond my intellectual capability and yet that dream would show me something I never expected. When I asked God for angelic wings for my jockeys to fly home I got sweet F***k all and yet when I least expected it came in a dream.
I haven't had one since mind and I still live in hope that to have a dream where you are given the name of the horse that wins, well it's every punters dream come true isn't it? Anyway back to the serious stuff night after night I began to cross-reference my books taking notes on this, notes on that, formulating a picture, a much distorted one but nevertheless a picture. My first interest was in the spiritism and the channelling so that was the basis of all my investigative work. I looked to see if there was any connection to spirits, the occult or mysticism in any way shape or form whilst researching. Nowadays it is much easier researching things with the computer etc but I didn't have one then, so it was very hard work. My gut feeling was that eventually if I searched hard enough and persevered long enough, I would indeed find clarity in the long search. Just where the next clue would come from in my search I could never be sure, perhaps from a book, perhaps from my guides (inner voices) but it always came. I had recently purchased a book called 'John Dee' by Peter French. I discovered Dee was heavily into the occult so he had to be central to any investigation. Dee had many friends in high places and one in

particular was a certain Lord Strange or Ferdinando Stanley the fifth Earl of Derby. He held some worthy interest for me. For not only did Lord Strange visit Dee's house for séances and studied the Occult under Dee, but for many years he was also a theatrical patron. Titus Andronicus the Shakespeare play had been originally written for Strange as shown in its title page. Later, I was to discover Lord Strange had a company of actors, who amalgamated with the Burbage theatre. After Strange`s rather suspicious death, Lord Hunsden the Queen's cousin patronised the Burbage actors and called them The Lord Chamberlain's men. What came with Burbage was a link to the Globe, Shakespeare's theatre and a link between Dee and Shakespeare via Lord Strange. I also discovered that the Globe theatre was built with much astrological symbolism in mind. I quickly realised that finding connections from Dr Dee wasn't too difficult, after all he was a central figure around Queen Elizabeth the 1st's time, but I was looking for links to tie in with the world I understood, the world of mysticism and channelling. I became absolutely fascinated with the Elizabethan era and its characters. And Shakespeare and his friends were becoming not only a source of great enjoyment for me in unfolding a mystery, but also essential for my understanding 'in search of the swan'.

# CHAPTER EIGHT

### *ALL ROADS LEAD TO FRANCE*

Taking a break from the intense research and I had been with Isabelle just a few months when we visited France for the second occasion. We went to visit Isabelle's grandmother who lived in La Ferte Bernard some 30 minutes drive from Le Mans. Mimi, a lovely old lady, greeted me. Isabelle asked if I would give Mimi some healing on a shoulder complaint that had descended on her in recent times. I happened to notice that she never moved her hand from an apron pocket. Perhaps it has affected her arm I thought? With Isabelle as an interpreter Mimi was asked to sit down, (Her hand still within the confines of the pocket). "Now then Mimi tell me how can I help?" She looked completely bemused as if an alien had landed in her front room. "It's ok, I won't bite!" I took hold of her left hand to reassure her. This brought a smile to her face "that's better, now which shoulder is it?" I asked. Before getting the reply I placed my hands on the left one." "It's the lef' (breaking conversation in mid-sentence). "Ah you knew!" said Isabelle (looking surprised). I administered healing in my usual way, hands placed on the head first. Feeling nothing in particular during the healing, I watched as a rather peculiar expression came over Mimi's face when I said, "I am also going to help your hand as well!" It was then that I discovered the reason for the hand in the apron. Her hand had not moved for some 47 years due to some form of shock she had suffered in her thirties. "It's not possible to help with that" replied Mimi rather dismissively. I grinned and said "anything is possible believe me." Within minutes of healing the hand showed signs of life. There were gasps from the people there and Mimi almost fainted as digit-by-digit the hand showed signs of working. Within half an hour the hand, which was whiter than Queen Elizabeth the first's face, turned pink! Mimi turned the hand slowly but surely and movement returned although not to full capacity it was pretty remarkable. She was delighted and astonished with what she had witnessed she told Isabelle. We had all agreed it was a miracle and unexplainable. I left the house feeling in awe of the powers that blessed me that day and returned to the peace and the tranquility of mind as I went home to rest. Mimi certainly had no placebo effect neither did Ronald when he had his healing bless him. The only thing Mimi was concerned with was would it stop her benefits! Having enjoyed my second trip to France in weeks I felt refreshed and full of the joys of spring. I eventually met Sandy and a good friend she turned out to be to both myself and Isabelle. Isabelle's meeting Sandy that day had enabled me to meet Patrick from the bookshop. Synchronicity is such an amazing thing. And no I don't believe in coincidence any more. How can you?

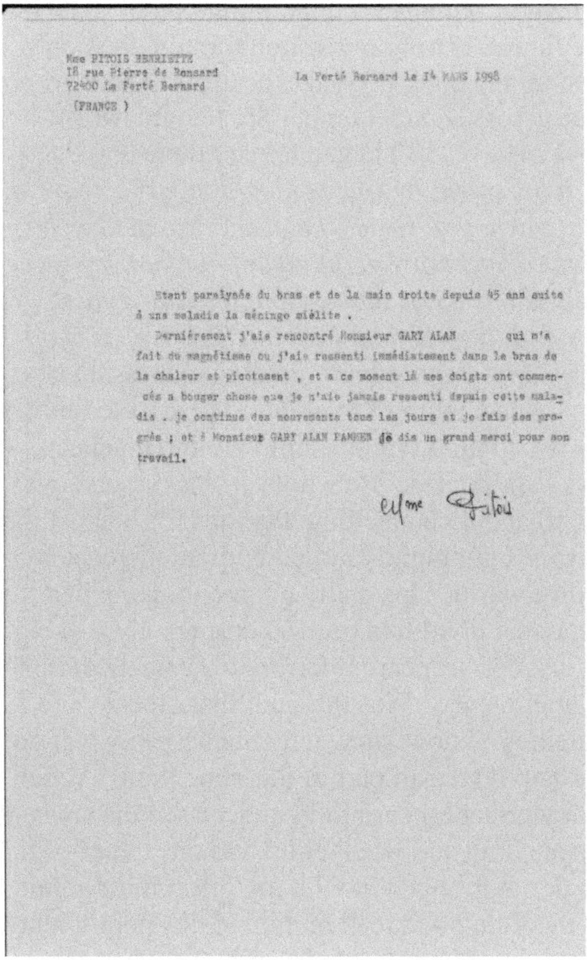

Mme PITOIS HENRIETTE
18 rue Pierre de Ronsard
72400 La Ferté Bernard
(FRANCE )

La Ferté Bernard le 14 MARS 1998

Etant paralysée du bras et de la main droite depuis 45 ans suite à une maladie la méningo miélite .

Dernièrement j'ais rencontré Monsieur GARY ALAN qui m'a fait du magnétisme ou j'ais ressenti immédiatement dans le bras de la chaleur et picotement , et a ce moment là mes doigts ont commencés a bouger chose que je n'aie jamais ressenti depuis cette maladie . je continue des mouvements tous les jours et je fais des progrès ; et à Monsieur GARY ALAN FAMMER je dis un grand merci pour son travail.

Mme Pitois

*Letter of thanks from Madame Pitois*

Feeling bored one night I thought better get back to some research so I placed all the relevant books I had obtained since the quest began on the table and spread them out like a pack of cards. I took a pen and paper and began to jot down all manner of information. Things I thought might be of some use in the future. During my search through the books I picked up the book of Shakespeare's sonnets, where I came across sonnet number 86. I could hardly believe my eyes as I began to read down the lines *'Was it his spirit, by spirits taught to write above a mortal pitch, that struck me dead? No, neither he, nor his compeers by night giving him aid, my verse astonished. He, nor that affable familiar ghost which nightly gulls him with intelligence, as victors of my silence cannot boast*'. My goodness, that refers to channelling I thought. That affable familiar ghost which nightly gulls him with intelligence, Wow! Just like Dee! So whoever Shakespeare was knew all about channelling. Perhaps it's a ghost that gulls me? I got nightly gulled with intelligence by the spirit world. This really got me thinking that this was the real link I had been so desperately seeking. Who was Shakespeare referring to as being gulled with intelligence? Was the said Shakespeare channelling? I now knew why Shakespeare was so important. It was all part of the same thing. At the very least Shakespeare fully understood the concept of channelling and whether he was the author of the plays or not it linked in with my gift. I must admit from the little I had read on him at this point I had my doubts to the authenticity of him as the great bard. Sonnet 86 and its description made me wonder if Dr Dee was the person being referred to in the piece. But then I thought well they had no TV or radio then so channelling must have been much more commonplace than it is today. So Shakespeare could have been referring to any number of people but that is unimportant really the fact that he mentions channelling though is. One thing for certain Shakespeare (whoever he may been) was talking about channelling a subject close to John Dee's heart and one he was commensurate with. Nearly all Shakespeare's work had some supernatural content but sonnet 86 gave me something tangible. It meant that Shakespeare was no longer just a writer of great vivid imagination when it came to the supernatural, but ONE WHO KNOWS! The only contemporary reference to the actor Shakespeare that could be called biographical, found among Jonson's papers after his death in 1637 and printed in *Discoveries* in 1641, is the following comment:- 'I *remember,* the Players have often mentioned it as an honour to *Shakespeare,* that in his writing, (whatsoever he penn'd) hee never blotted out line. My answer hath beene, Would he had blotted a thousand. Which they thought a malevolent speech. I had not told posterity this, but for their ignorance, who choose that circumstance to commend their friend by, wherein he most faulted. And to justifie mine owne candor, (for I lov'd the man, and doe honour his memory (on this side Idolatry) as much as any.) Hee was (indeed) honest, and of an open, and free nature: had an excellent *Phantsie;* brave notions, and gentle expressions: wherein hee flow'd with that facility, that sometime it was necessary he should be stop'd: I found the above very interesting as it refers to Shakespeare 'never having blotted out a line' something I never do when channelling. What started out a sonnet reading from Ronald had become like a bloody war and peace novel. Why had I met these different people along my way? What was their real purpose? What had led me, a boy who grew up in Stratford East to Shakespeare of all people? My journey had been full of synchronicity but at long last I could feel the answer was imminent. It was like looking for a needle in a haystack at the beginning but I knew the answer was there somewhere, drawing ever closer and one day soon I would find it. Some very strange things happened during this period one in particular showed me another side to the power of this energy. One evening whilst at Margaret's her daughter's boyfriend all 6ft 3" of him was ridiculing spirit whilst I was in full flow, much to my annoyance! Then as if by some great hand of fate he collapsed holding his chest. After a few minutes, he got up aided by his friends. He admitted he was taking the pi** and was very sorry. He would never doubt again. Well done the spirit that struck him down!

In the summer of 1998 I took a trip to South Kensington and it was in a shop nearby the tube station that I met a lady named Freddie. I told her I was looking for the college of psychic studies which I knew was in the vicinity somewhere.
She informed me she had no idea where it was but told me she had an interest in such things and would like to know more about them. She said she was 'fascinated' by the subject. "Why don't we have a coffee and a chat, I have a bit of time." "Great!" "later today perhaps?" "Why not now?" she asked. "Fine" I replied, let's go." We walked a few yards and entered a local coffee bar. The coffee was awful if my memory serves me right but the conversation proved stimulating. After an hour or so a friend of Freddie's walked in. I remember thinking the lady

rather eccentric but there was something about her I couldn't quite figure out. “This is my friend Sheila Gary, she channels!” Ah! That’s it I thought! But before the word ‘hi’ came out from my mouth, she was gone like the wind. Charming I thought, she could have had a quick chat. I carried on conversing with Freddie for a little longer then left myself.
I met Freddie for coffee on two more occasions within three months of the initial meeting and low and behold like a bad penny on each occasion Sheila turned up. On the third occasion she gave me her business card “call if you want” she said rather abruptly. I felt it odd how we should keep bumping into each other and decided to take a chance and give her a call. I had the feeling Freddie would be just another catalyst for the meeting of Sheila and so it proved. Sheila and I met some weeks later at a cafe in Holland Park. I realised that our meeting on those three separate occasions was much more than coincidence, more a synchronistic happening.
We got on like a house on fire and quickly established a rapport. Freddie God bless her went back to her normal life but Sheila was just beginning to become part of mine. A story she told me had me more than fascinated. 14 years previous she had seen a therapist and the therapist had told Sheila she had seen an image of a swan! A swan I said excitedly. “The swan is the animal which I keep coming across. We must be linked but how and why?” What was it with this swan thing? Firstly me being told to write a book called ‘In search of the swan’, Shakespeare (sweet Swan of Avon), my Letter from Deborah M referring to a swan, the swan being the animal symbol for the Kether in the Kabbalistic teaching, a section of the Templars

known as the 'Knights of the Swan' and Sheila! Was this swan all part of the selfsame thing? Was this swan something universal I began to wonder? Sheila was as baffled as me, but like me she never had a clue of its relevance. That is if there was any in the first place. Nevertheless she felt like me that it had to be something, it just had to be. Sheila it appeared had replaced my dear friend Ronald, slightly younger and more beautiful (Only kidding if you're listening Ron). Once again I had ears that truly listened. After countless meetings and discussions Sheila too went in search of the understanding of the swan and soon developing an interest in Shakespeare along the way. Like me Sheila loved old books and we spent many an hour sifting through the book shelves in book shops. The desire for understanding became a need rather than a pleasure. It was an Investigation that seemed to have no end. Research and study had taken my life over. At least with Sheila as a support it made the search and research a little easier. Don't think I have enjoyed every moment of my learning because I haven't. It has been terribly hard at times, but if the body is willing and the mind is strong, mountains can be moved. My mountains have been few but within myself was the biggest mountain of all. All I needed to move was my mountain and find that swan swimming somewhere out there in the ether. I had a truly remarkable experience and something which proved meeting Isabelle was destiny. My 'All roads lead to France' would have a very magical significance. I was on my way back from France and sitting on the ferry. I turned to see a lady sitting behind me. I turned to Isabelle and said "I will talk to that lady in a minute." "Oh no" she said “Not another of your psychic intrusions” “Oh yes” I then turned to the lady behind me. “Hi, where have you been in France?” “A beautiful little town staying with a friend” she replied. “I felt I had to talk to you. I often get a feeling to talk to people if there is a reason” “Oh, she said. Then I mentioned that I have a passion for Shakespeare and someone called Dr John Dee.” “Really, well, isn’t that strange? My son Nicholas is studying John Dee just at this moment” What are the odds of meeting a lady on a ferry whose son is studying a 16th century Alchemist? Now that is spooky. John Dee is hardly everyone’s topic of conversation. “Let me give you Nicholas` telephone number, which she did. Jane and I became very good friends thereinafter. I contacted Nicholas and told him about his mother’s and my remarkable meeting. I told him about my interest in Dee and Shakespeare and he suggested we meet which we did. After a most enjoyable meeting Nicolas gave me a book to read called ‘The Holy blood and Holy Grail’. “Read this” he said. 3 months or so later I returned the book to Nicolas, “I could not get around to reading it mate” I said. “Shame, good book that” he replied. Remarkably after handing the book back within two weeks three copies had come my way. One turned up in an Oxford bookshop whilst I was in there browsing the shelves with Sheila. One then turned up in a Norfolk bookshop (my purpose being in Norfolk is revealed later in the book) some two weeks later in which Margaret did exactly the same as Sheila had done two weeks previous, she handed me a book from nowhere and said “I feel you should buy this” “what is it?” I asked “it’s something called “Holy Blood and the Holy Grail.” Bloody hell it must be a sign, I should read it! One week later I was certain I should as the local Oxfam shop yielded me yet another copy! What its contents were I knew not. A month later I went off to Le Mans for a much needed break, armed with a copy of 'The Holy Blood and Holy Grail' this time I was going to read it. The sun was shining and I was sitting in Isabelle's family's garden armed with a glass of fruit juice in one hand and the book in the other. Relaxed and enjoying a thoroughly entertaining read. I arrived at page 155 about Charles Nodier and his circle. During the French revolution Napoleon ordered the Vatican be raided with an ambition to create the definitive library. Almost all the contents of the Vatican archives were plundered and removed to Paris. Nodier, Eliphas Levi and Jean Baptiste Pitois were given the task at the Arsenal library to sift through the plundered documents and books. I nearly choked on my drink because Pitois is the name of Isabelle's family and that name is not a common name in France. Could he have been related I wondered, now that would be amazing. As I read further it said that Pitois had a non de plume of Paul Christian and he had written a book called the 'Histoire de la Magie' published in 1870. It is a book that had now become a coveted work amongst the students of the occult. I decided to see if I could find anything about it. Isabelle's brother Stephane then walked in. "Have a look in this bookshop" he said handing me a bookmark. "It has many spiritual books and old books perhaps they will help you?" Le Mans has a population of only around 300,000 and as for bookshops they are sparse indeed. I took the bookmark and noted the shop name l'athanor, 22 rue marchande. "Drop me off there tomorrow please Isabelle if you would be so kind" that she did. I found the small bookshop in

the heart of town and it had many books cluttered together. The owner was busying himself tidying the books so I decided to browse the vast occult section. I then purchased eight books on various subjects and hoped to find something on Pitois.
I asked the owner about Pitois but he said he knew nothing of him. I took the books home and on inspecting them all found nothing on the man, much to my disappointment. I telephoned the bookshop and asked the owner if he would take one of the books back I had bought. "No problem" he replied. "Please bring me that name again when you come in and I will look it up for you and see if there are any books on him, please come tomorrow after 10am." I returned to the shop and took with me the book to return plus the Holy Blood and Grail book. On arriving I handed the unwanted book back and showed him the book I had. I turned to Page 155 and as I started to read the passage he listened intently. "Jean Baptiste Pitois alias Paul Christian" "Ah, my God. I have a book of Christian in my private collection." He returned after five minutes with the book. "Here it is, The Histoire De La Magie 1870" I nearly died. "That's amazing" I said. He then opened the book and showed me a print inside of an alchemist. He then pointed to the wall behind me and low and behold the print had been copied and was on his wall. "I have had it there for three years" he added. That print is only in that book, nowhere else not even in English re-issues is it to be found. He then handed me a paper bag with the print on it as well. I have had these done one year ago" I was amazed. The odds of this happening must be a billion to one chance! It proved to me that not only was Isabelle and I destined to meet but my life was destined. L'athanor actually means

'The Alchemist's Furnace' and this indeed was some magical, magical alchemy. I still have the bag the owner gave me of the print and it is in a frame at home. Sure roof and indeed a reminder of that magical synchronicity. We still have to discover whether Pitois is related in some way but my guess is it is welcome to the family!

*L'athanor Bookshop in Le Mans, France*

*Print of the alchemist from the shop*

*Title page from the book Histoire de la Magie - Paul Christian 1870*

# CHAPTER NINE

## *THE DISCOVERY*

After returning from my amazing trip to France it was back to rainy old Britain. My search now had now fully focused on Francis Bacon a Lawyer by profession. Also a Philosopher, Statesman, Writer, member of Parliament and son of Nicolas Bacon. According to the book of Melsome there are countless parallelisms between the works of Bacon and the works of Shakespeare. And it is said 'Shakespeare' borrowed extensively from Francis Bacon's De Augmentis Scientiarum which was not published before 1623 and by then Shakespeare had been dead seven years! I hadn't a clue whether it was right or wrong and frankly didn't care. My interest was trying to connect the channelling etc with all and sundry of the era. And to see if, the Shakespeare enigma had a truth behind its apparent mask. Shortly after studying the Melsome book I received a call from my friend Patrick at the bookshop in Surrey. He told me he had something for me that might be of interest. He said he hadn't a clue what the book contained only that the title was The Secret Shakespeare by Alfred Dodd. The title had drawn his attention. He went on to say that it was an old book and that I just might find something to assist my research. Two days later the book safely arrived.  I opened the package to find a rather small book. The title indeed seemed interesting 'The Secret Shake-Speare' by Alfred Dodd. I opened the cover and noticed straight away a reference to Freemasonry. I'd forgotten the Freemasonry aspect but was fascinated upon

reading Dodd like Melsome also believed Bacon to have been Shakespeare. How could it be that I was now in possession of two very old books both at least fifty years old both saying that Shakespeare and Bacon were the same and with both books coming from Patrick within a short space of time of one another. It appeared like more synchronicity. Whereas the Melrose book dealt with the parallelism the work of Shakespeare and Bacon, Dodd tells of the coded messages within the works of Shakespeare. I read that Melsome had described Bacon as 'The profoundest thinker of his age' and he was not on his own in such high praise of Bacon, there were many. On his death 32 letters of praise were dedicated to him in the Manes Verulamini. One thing became very clear Bacon had far more to him than I first realised. His Rosicrucian links were starting to manifest in my understanding. The Rose Cross was a secret fraternity. Bacon I found went to the Temple Church in London as a youth and there began his passion for the Knights Templar.
The Church built by the Knights Templar has effigies of the Pembroke's inside. I realised the letter 'Dr Dee to Mr Shakespeare' unearthed at the local studies library in Richmond Old Town Hall was Masonic and 'Foucault's pendulum' Umberto Eco was along those lines too, as to was the Great Law by Hamish Machuisdean another book Geraldine had come across. All these books and sources of information were leading towards a Masonic thinking. The Hiram Key by Lomas & Knight and the Templar Revelation by Picknett and Prince were other books that helped my understanding. Within days of obtaining these books a television documentary of the Templars

appeared and I sat glued to my set. The programme was very relevant to the books I had just obtained. It was all fascinating stuff. My search that had started with that Shakespeare sonnet of Ronald's was now in full flight. A book I read even described the first folio of Shakespeare as the biggest Masonic book ever written! The play the Tempest and Loves Labours lost in particular had much reference to Masonic things. The programme I had watched on the Templars had such a profound impact on me, so much so that the next thing I knew I was in the Church of Notre Dame in Leicester square puzzling over a mural seen on the Templar programme, of Jean Cocteau. It was all very mysterious indeed. 'Look at the feet' a voice in my head said. I looked at the feet in the mural to see a rose and the feet were crossed, 'Rose Cross'. It was all very symbolic. Three weeks later as part of the journey of discovery I was in Paris walking around St Sulpice and entering the famous church there. A Church where the Priest Sauniere of Rennes le Chateau fame had stood more than a century earlier. All roads lead to France was beginning to sound very prophetic. Perhaps I would live there at some point in the future? My trip to the church and Paris had been truly inspirational and a future visit to Rennes le Chateau simply a must.

The Elizabethan era really resonates with me and reading one book about Shakespeare gave me the answer to where Shakespeare was described as the swan. An attributation to William Shakespeare. Ben Jonson's tribute to Shakespeare in the first folio 1623 entitled:

***TO SHAKESPEARE AND WHAT HE HATH LEFT US***

*As brandish`t at the eyes of ignorance,*
*Sweet swan of Avon! What a sight it were*
*To see thee in our water yet appeare,*
*And make those flights upon the bankes of Thames,*
*That so did take Eliza and our James!*
***B**ut stay, I see thee in the hemisphere*
***A**dvanced, and made a **Con**stellation there!*
***S**hine forth, thou starre of poets, and with rage*
***O**r influence, chide or cheere the drooping stage:*
***W**hich, since thy flight fro` hence,*
*hath mourn`d like night,*
*And despairs day, but for thy volumes light.*

What I found so fascinating about this piece by Ben Jonson is that Avon is Celtic for a river but if that is reversed it thus it becomes Nova a bright star. Reference to 'thou star of poets' in Jonson's piece had me wondering. The reference to stars got me looking at the subject of Astrology. As another man a certain astronomer named Simon Studion. Studion was a Wittenberg theologian who had influence and a following for his enlightenment teachings and observations of things astrological in the late 1500's and early 1600's. Studion was a prominent German Rosicrucian and Francis Bacon was also a Rosicrucian who had much influence in Germany after he took his teaching there. Studion's influence increased when a supernova occurred in

(wait for it) the constellation of Cygnus the Swan in 1604. The term it's written in the stars may just be apt in this case. Cygnus, Avon, Swan, Nova, star of poets and not forgetting the word Constellation very interesting. I looked at the tribute of Ben Jonson carefully and then noticed something. By using a system of ciphers if you take in line six first letter is a 'B' directly below on line seven is an 'A' in the sentence is the word CONstellation which spells out Bacon. What rubbish I hear you shout! But wait directly below Line eight begins with 'S' line nine begins with an 'O' and line ten begins with a 'W' which spells SOW and a sow is a female pig and a pig is Bacon. Dodd points out in his book 'Secret Shakespeare' that Sow is a Masonic term used for son of wisdom and that certainly fits Bacon.
It certainly seemed to validate what Dodd had said about the ciphers. I was sure the ones I had found were correct. I was also certain there are many others waiting to be found. It didn't prove Bacon was Shakespeare and I don't believe he is but the vein of truth in which the mystical road I was travelling was connecting to these great men meant I could get a little excited!

My life was certainly to change on this particular day with books piled up on the dining table. Paper scattered like snowflakes. Pencils and pens crossed as if in combat, it looked a bloody mess. Oh God I thought can't be bothered with all this, then the phone rang it was Isabelle "I'm pregnant" she said, "I'm fainting," I said. How did it happen? Reality dawned. Gary it's yours! You are going to be a daddy. Nappies and all! Oh no. It can't be possible? My road led to France all right, not only on the bloody ferry but becoming part of it. And then just nine months later the wonderful arrival (not as hoped on Shakespeare's birthday 23rd of April though!) but baby arrived on the 8th of May at 23 hours and four minutes! Nine and a half pounds and it's a boy. I was there at the birth and what an incredible moment that was… tears of joy, anticipation and fear as baby arrived, and then holding him in my arms for the first time, a living creation. It was a most amazing, amazing experience.

A couple of weeks later we arrived at the Registrars office. The Registrar armed with pen in hand. "You are number 46 on the certificate. What is the child's name?" Adam John William. Adam for the first man. John for John Dee and William for Shakespeare. What about Francis in honour of Bacon? Don't like the name Francis. "That's funny said the lady" "What the name?" "No silly" she replied. "Your cheque is also the number 46!"
A week later full of the joys of fatherhood I met up with Sheila in London. "Sheila, we called the baby, Adam." "Never! That's incredible my son is also named Adam!" She then went on to show me a book about the Knights Templars. A certain King Baldwin II who had given the island of Malta to a Knights Templar called I'lle de'Adam. The surgeon who delivered baby Adam was called Baldwin!
Oh it's getting silly now! I never saw baby in the tea leaves and wasn't best pleased with my guides (inner voices). What now? Armed with piles or research and a baby! "Here is a present for you" said Sheila "what is it?" "The King James Bible" "I had just been reading about that Sheila funnily enough." I discovered that Francis Bacon had a hand in the putting the together of the King James

Bible of 1611. Oddly the 46th word from the top of the psalm 46 is Shake and the 46th word from the bottom was Spear, Shakespeare (albeit the word Selah) The KJ Bible was completed in 1610 when Shakespeare's age would have been 46 and the committee who oversaw the Bible consisted of 46 members. Goodness me! Strange but true. I never thought from what I had read about Shakespeare that one man could have written the works of Shakespeare, so saying it was Bacon didn't equate either but a group with the same interests appealed to me with Bacon as a major player. So many people could have had a hand in the works in theory that it was take your pick. Obviously Shakespeare from my findings couldn't have written all the works. Was he part of a group? Was channelling from the spirits part of it all? My channelling proves you can be a number of different people with only you as the author. It is possible. Life is all too brief but at least having seen Ulla Ronald's wife in spirit form I knew that death wasn't the finality anymore but a gateway to some other dimension, some other realm.
There are indeed more things in heaven than earth methinks! Perhaps his knowledge derived from where mine did the spirit world? I was relatively uneducated yet wrote material far beyond my capability so it is an idea that couldn't be ruled out. Dee along with Lord Strange, Sir Francis Walsingham, Sir Phillip Sidney, Giordano Bruno along with many others from Shakespeare's era, were all interested in the occult (which simply means hidden). In fact a mysterious school of night existed with Strange, Walter Raleigh, Henry Percy, Christopher Marlowe, *Chapman*, Roydon, Hariot and others. It seems the influential Dee had a considerable hand in things with his immense occult

knowledge. Perhaps a group with a common denominator, an interest at heart contributed to the works of Shakespeare with playwrights, Poets, Philosophers, Occultists and Classical Scholars all having fun putting thoughts, words and actions together 'Shaking a Spear' at the world? It is interesting to note that Francis Bacon when at Grays Inn at the temple in London heart of the Law schools in his younger days, belonged to 'the order of the helmet' an invisible knighthood dedicated to Pallas Athena (the shaker of the spear). And another thing I found of interest was from a book by Anthony Aldridge called 'Shakespeare and the Prince of Love' he points out that Shakespeare's Twelfth Night was commissioned for performance in 1602 in the middle temple hall in the heartland of Bacon's law study. It is also near that fabulous Temple Church built by the Templars and where effigies of the Pembroke family are. The Earl of Pembroke makes a dedication in Shakespeare's first folio. The works of Shakespeare have survived almost five centuries and so little is known of the author it's amazing! Having already linked Shakespeare's work with the channelling in sonnet 86, as previously mentioned it seemed a network of well-established people were all interlinked whether by family or by friend including Bacon.
It reads like a who's who! I wanted to find a connection between Bacon and Shakespeare.
I found the connection in the shape of a Mr Whitgift. Dean Whitgift as he was known was Bacon's tutor whilst he was at Cambridge, like Dee was to Bacon he was also a mentor and he was also Bacon's friend. What intrigued me was the same Mr Whitgift authorised the marriage license for Mr Shakespeare and who paved the way for Venus and

Adonis to be published, a play who some believe Bacon himself wrote. I could probably write a book on just the connections but if readers search for themselves a wealth of information is available.
I am not a Baconian, Marlowevian, Shakesfordian or Oxfordian for that matter. They all appear to have been involved in the writing of Shakespeare's works in some way but there is always one reason or the other why they could not possibly be the sole author. Shakespeare works with its enormous input from the world of mysticism implies that the minds of those like Dee or any great occult minded individuals were certainly involved or influential in the collation of the first folio of Shakespeare. Those who were bringers of the occult and knowledge from friendly familiar ghosts were burned or many other unthinkable things by puritans and those opposed to the truth. They were persecuted for being heretical. The content of Shakespeare's work tells far more than the person whose name adorns the first folio of 1623 that's for certain. From what I had read from the two authors who came out on the side of Bacon had enormous weight behind their theories, but I needed to look further and deeper. The Earl of Oxford, The Earl of Northumberland, The Earl of Pembroke, The Earl of Southampton, The Earl of Essex, The Earl of Rutland, Cecil, Manners, Beaumont, Fletcher and not Forgetting T.T or Thomas Thorpe, the list is endless but they all had their own little insight into Shakespeare. The Earl of Rutland for example studied in Padua, Italy. In particular records from 28 March 1596 show the names of his fellow students, Mr Rosencrantz and Mr Guildenstern. (Rose Croix and Golden Star to the initiated) Rutland also went to Elsinore queue Hamlet. This certainly provides a

distinct link to the play, Shakespeare and the Rosicrucians. There were so many theories, so many possibilities. Frankly I didn't care who wrote Shakespeare's work only about the content and message contained within it. Everything about Shakespeare's mystery was exciting for me, and every clue, every book I read, told me more. I was getting there for certain. Shakespeare's works are the second biggest seller of all time succeeded only by the Bible. Like the works of Shakespeare the Bible needs to be seen with fresh eyes. To study the Bible through allegorical astrological symbolism instead of reading as is, leads you to a completely different understanding. In Ben Jonson's play the alchemist he gives reference to the scriptures when he says they were often in parables, wrapped in perplexed allegories. I now knew that Shakespeare's works spoke a great truth and the need to see through allegory was so important.

In late 1999 Sheila had a strong feeling we should visit the theosophical Society in London." "Why?" I asked. "I just feel we should go there" she replied. "What's there then?" "I haven't the faintest" she replied. But following her Intuitive feeling we arrived at the Society in Gloucester Place W1. On arriving I enquired at the counter if they had any books on Shakespeare, perhaps on Freemasonry of some description? "Yes, over there on the top shelf." It was there I saw a book called 'The Hidden Life in Freemasonry' written by C.W Leadbeater. Wow! That looks interesting I thought. It proved more than that, for as I opened the back of the book I saw the contents and found on page 283 the word 'Hamsa' or the 'Swan'. What were the odds of finding that on that day? Simply astonishing!

I discovered that the word Hamsa was a Hindu word and that the 'Swan' is the third great step to spiritual enlightenment. "So that's what the swan is!" I delightedly said to Sheila that's incredible!
I now knew the whole purpose of my search for the swan was a search for 'enlightenment' and that Shakespeare had come into my life because that part of history was all about enlightenment too. To teach others that life is eternal. I do believe that the brain and mind are separate entities and not part of the selfsame thing. Simply because when the body dies the brain dies with it. And of course if it were how science believed it to be, then on death the mind would die too. If what I do is proven (and indeed it is) and you can communicate with the afterlife, then you must be communicating with mind after death. Thus proving the mind survives. So it can't be as we are taught. It simply can't! Science knows so little if anything about the mind. Understanding it from a new perspective gives opportunity for a new way of understanding, indeed it does!

# CHAPTER TEN

## *THE PHOTOGRAPH*

My relationship with Isabelle had by now sadly reached its inevitable conclusion and after 3 years it was sadly time to go our separate ways, but we had a beautiful son together which I wouldn't have changed for the world and now 'le chemin du destin' would take us in separate directions. As for the search now that the swan had been found and I knew exactly what my journey was I could relax from the hard work of research. Shakespeare and co could be put to rest or so I thought! Out of the blue a letter arrived from Norfolk. I don't know anyone in Norfolk I thought. I opened the letter and found inside a press cutting from the Norfolk press.
It proclaimed the Earl of Oxford is Shakespeare! Warner Brothers in America was paying big money for the rights of a book based on this theory.
What a waste of money I thought. The Earl of Oxford is Shakespeare methinks not! A contributor almost certainly, but the sole author never!

A couple of months passed and a thought voice entered telling me to reconnect with Margaret. I didn't have a clue where she was now. I hadn't seen her for over two years. I still had her daughter's number so gave her a ring. She telephoned me back and told me her mum had moved to you guessed it Norfolk! Ah, so it was Margaret who sent the press cutting. After being given Margaret's telephone number we then reconnected. Six months later I went to Norfolk to see her. Whilst there she had a strong feeling to invite someone she had met while living there over a man named Gerry Parish. "Gerry is coming this afternoon so I shall leave you two together when he comes." Gerry arrived mid afternoon. He has a fascination with BSE and believed he had the answer to how it derived. It was certainly an interesting theory. I really liked him. He had a passion like me about what he did. I told him how much I would have loved to have met Michael Bentine, once of the goons fame. "That is strange Gary" Why?" I asked "because I was just about to give you a website address I have and Michael Bentine was connected to it in some way before his death. Fantastic I thought. I then contacted Pharo.com and spoke to a man named Richard Taylor. After a series of emails I discovered Michael Bentine was indeed remembered fondly by those connected to the site. I then spoke to Nicolas the one who gave me the (Holy Blood & Holy Grail book) Jane's son who I met through meeting Jane on a ferry journey home from France. And told him all about Pharo and my connection with Gerry and he was eager to contact Richard. He did, low and behold surprise, surprise, Richard who was in Scotland at the time and Nicholas who was in Southampton had both gone to the same school in Surrey years back. So an amazing web was being built! I invited Gerry over to stay with me a couple of times and we had some amazing experiences. One in particular was too hard to believe but it happened. I started to talk and another voice was coming out of me. It was bizarre and what was even more bizarre was that the voice claimed to be that of the late Archbishop Runcie. He said many things which we took note of. When he had gone I went to the toilet I heard the words in my head the Duchy of Cornwall. "Who is the

Duchy of Cornwall Gerry?" "Prince Charles and Diana were married by Runcie." "Well I never!" We looked up Runcie on the web and discovered that all he had said could be verified. I knew absolutely nothing about him. Could this possibly be true? Could it really be Runcie from beyond the grave? Who knows? All I know is that whoever gave me the information said what he said, it was checked and proven correct. Other spirits who have come through and claimed to be someone famous or not, is all well and good but I reserve judgment until it is proven to me, and the only way you can do that is by the evidence given. The following day I and a few psychic friends were in a bookshop in central London. Sheila and John who were with me and Gerry both reached up to the same bookshelf and pulled a number of books down onto themselves. When the dust had settled, the book which was staring up at us all was 'The Prince and the Paranormal' the book about Charles and his Paranormal beliefs. Seeing that was absolutely amazing. Shortly after this Gerry then got a message from a medium on platform at Norwich spiritualist church and the medium told Gerry he had a message for him from Michael Bentine who had been the medium's friend during his lifetime. Later when I was writing a letter I too received a message from Michael Bentine. He told me he had a connection to Norwich, which in fact turned out to be correct. I have no doubt it was Michael, sounds impossible I know, but information the spirit gave was enough to convince us it was him. I later found out that the guys at Pharo well, Stephen Prior (the owner) in particular actually knew Michael Bentine very well and was with him at his passing. He had

kept in contact with his widow until sadly he himself died a few months after my meeting him. Michael Bentine was really gifted himself and saw his own son's demise in a plane crash. His son a keen flier was begged by Michael not to fly on this particular day but did so all the same sadly Michael's worst fears were realized and the plane crashed and his son was killed. Michael has come through a couple more times since and he wanted me to write a documentary script based on a subject dear to his heart based on a book by Bligh Bond called 'The Gate of Remembrance'. I once owned one of the original copies from 1918. It is a very well known book which certain priests had tried to destroy copies of because of its content. Michael Bentine like me also had a copy of the original book. The book based on channelled information that came through John Alleyne, Bligh Bond's friend who channelled material relating to Glastonbury Abbey from long dead monks.
On excavating the abbey the information given to Alleyne by the spirit monks proved to be accurate. It is an amazing story well worth a read.
Another strange tale was we once held meetings of likeminded people at the Henley tearooms. On this particular day I had a copy of Michael Bentine's book 'A Door Marked Summer' with me. A new member came that day to join us and clasped in her hand was you've guessed it a copy of 'A Door Marked Summer' bizarre! What are the odds on that? Her name was Marilyn, we became good friends thereafter. She told me she had met Michael Bentine some years back who had signed her book personally and gave her a wonderful message at wait for it `The Swan Theatre'. I said to Marilyn "next time that this group meets there will be only

seven of us!" She looked surprised because the group had grown regularly. Sure enough when we met some four weeks later there was only seven. The group disbanded shortly after. Marilyn and I stayed friends and took a trip up to Edinburgh to the Templar Lodge hotel home of Stephen Prior and Pharo. We had a fantastic time up there and took a trip to Roslyn chapel, which was just twenty or so minutes from the hotel. Roslyn is a magnificent building full of Templar history and the energy inside was rather breathtaking. As I entered the door you could sense its history and at one part of the Church I had a vision of a massacre with bodies falling and at another part of the Church I felt a chill that got colder and colder until I went through the arch of a room towards the right of the church at the far end. As I entered through the chill disappeared. I tried the experiment again by retracing my steps but the cold sensation never returned. I felt an eerie presence that day. If you get the chance visit Roslyn, it's a part of the wondrous historical past and a Templar historical site for all to enjoy. Although this was my first visit to Roslyn it would not be my last!

I do enjoy getting messages through from 'spirit' but the messages you get are not always what you want to hear. Nothing taught me that more than a message I received whilst doing the mundane washing up some weeks after. 'Gerry's dying' the voice in mind said 'can't be' I thought. I telephoned him later that evening. "Are you ok Gerry?" "Fine!" he replied. "No problems at all mate, just a little arthritis in my leg, nothing really!" We talked about all and sundry and it left me wondering why I had had that message during the day. It was so clear.

I thought Gerry you are not right at all. Two days later I received a call from Gerry's wife Rema. Her voice quaking with emotion she told me Gerry had been told earlier in the day he was suffering from stomach cancer. The prognosis was not good at all. My dear friend was going to die not if but when. Was it days, weeks, months? Intuition told me three months and so it proved to be. What grieved me was like me he had a passion. Mine was my gifts, and his the work with BSE. I would see my work completed whereas Gerry would fall at the last hurdle in life's race, bloody typical! Unless of course I fall before my race is won. Now I would be p****d off if that happened. You can't describe the feelings that go on inside of you knowing that someone close to you is going to have to go through hell. If there were a God why would my dear friend have to suffer in that horrendous way? Dear Ronald was off this mortal coil faster than the euro star and yet Gerry would endure the most hideous of deaths. Slow and torturous, it was so unfair. It was during this unfortunate time for Gerry that my life took an unexpected turn. I met a lady called Jan in Norwich at Ottakers bookshop. I began telling her things about her life and told her if she came to me for healing I could help. She did come to me for help. Three months later she told me her health had improved dramatically through the healing she had received. I was shocked to learn she had Multiple Sclerosis but was glad the healing had given her enormous benefit. We became good friends and one day I invited Jan to come and stay with me at my London home for a few days. Whilst there Jan talked of how she had met a blonde lady called Shona at some awareness class. "You don't like blondes do you Gary?" "Prefer Brunettes!"

I replied. As we talked I received a thought voice message Shona has a red car that pulls to the left. She also has a brother and is in a relationship that is going nowhere fast. Would you know if this is true Jan? "No, I couldn't tell you. I will telephone her tonight and you can ask her yourself" "Ok, I will." Later that night Jan telephoned Shona and put me on the telephone. I asked Shona about the red car and she confirmed she did indeed have a red car that pulled to left and was also in a relationship that was floundering and that in fact I was the forth psychic to tell her the relationship was doomed to failure. I gave Shona my email address and said that if she ever needed to speak to feel free to contact me. That evening I sat at my computer with Jan beside me. I had received an email from Shona with an attachment. On clicking the attachment a picture of Shona appeared before me. "Blimey Jan that is the girl I am going to marry!" "Good grief" she said. "Yes, that is definitely the one. I telephoned my Mother shortly afterwards and told her I had seen the girl I was going to marry. "Where did you meet?" "No, we haven't met! I have only seen a picture of her." "Oh for God's sake" she replied. My mother had no faith in my abilities. Goodness knows what my dad thought! I know deep down they believed me really. I was also told that night the date I would be married which was the 23rd of April 2004 and the date of the engagement would be 14th February 2003. During the next few days I was told by my inspired thought voice that not only was I going to marry Shona but that I would get engaged in Roslyn chapel (the place only weeks earlier I had gone with Marilyn) proposing with a red rose in hand with a ring placed in the centre. This just 3 months since first seeing the picture!

Not only that but I would be dressed as a Knights Templar in a medieval wedding too. Oh my God! This is unreal I thought. Although I had seen a picture of Shona she had no idea what I looked like. I sent a picture of Shakespeare to her which she found amusing. Now if this happens then I will say that my life is destined, it must be. Within a few days I travelled up to Norwich to see my dying friend Gerry and whilst there met up with Shona. Holding the hand of a dying man is one you never forget. How could I celebrate my good news when my friend was lying in the bed dying? I also had to try not to get too carried away by telling Shona I would be the one to marry her. With not even having had a single date that would be ludicrous. She might not find me the least bit attractive, what then? A don't even go there scenario. We went for a drink and there seemed as much possibility of romance by the end of the evening as me being struck by lightning zilch! I questioned the information I had received from the spirit guides (inner voices) and they repeated that it was my fate and that it would all take place. They were so insistent they suggested I booked two flights to Edinburgh for Valentine's Day and that I buy a rather expensive platinum diamond solitaire. What idiot would follow those instructions? Yes, you are right ME. I bought two return flights to Edinburgh airport for a trip over the Valentine's day period and a platinum solitaire diamond ring. What is wrong with you man? You haven't even been on a date! How do you know she fancies you? The odds of it all becoming reality from just seeing a picture to marriage was remote to say the least. Some have said 'well, you saw a picture of a beautiful girl. That is what most men would have wanted'. That may be true but it isn't just what I want is it? They also wondered if I had taken leave of my senses? Well, one might have thought so, but within a couple weeks, me and Shona was sending each other emails, that I suppose one could have induced were erring on the side of a possible romance? (Well, ok that was just me clutching at straws). I still hadn't told her of my inspired message. I was treading on eggshells still desperate to find out one way or the other if my spirit guides (inner voices) had got it right. Or was this a wind up of monumental proportions?

*The Photo of Shona that began it all*

One phone call just two months after the initial contact from Shona finally broke the ice. Shona had visions herself including firstly seeing two swans in a heart shape (swans again) and then a ring being placed in a red rose. She said she knew that I knew. "I know what?" I asked. "I know you are going to marry me" she replied. I could have collapsed. It was true. I even found out that at that the awareness class where she first met Jan, Shona was the very first person to attend that day, Jan was the second.

A class of around 30 attended. During the class they did a psychometry experiment. An item from each person there was placed on the table and each person was to pick an item, and by touch alone, tell someone something about them from their item without knowing who the item belonged too. Jan spoke to Shona and told her she would be putting in a gold watch of hers. So Shona avoided any watches so as not to get what Jan put in and picked a ring instead. From the ring Shona picked up intuitively that someone was feeling unwell and had images of a hospital in her mind. She later discovered the ring she had chosen belonged to Jan who had changed her mind about which item to use. Jan confirmed she had been feeling unwell and had a hospital appointment that day. All part of that amazing synchronicity that had brought us together and their meeting just one week before Jan came to visit me in London. Within weeks Shona and I were living together. We got engaged at Roslyn chapel in Edinburgh on Valentine's Day 2003. Just 3 months after I first saw her picture. Absolutely unbelievable! Not even one single date and yet we were engaged and living together. It was just incredible how much we had in common from politics to classical music, history you name it. Mind you the relationship fell down somewhat when she said he hated football. Oh well, can't have everything I suppose. The one downside was my friend Gerry never did get to see my happiness. I shall never forget my sweet friend who knew he was at death's door and showed enormous courage and dignity. Like Ronald he had gone to play with the angels.

# CHAPTER ELEVEN

## *THE SWAN IS FOUND*

Valentine's Day soon approached and I had two flights tickets Edinburgh. Would this whirlwind romance fizzle and bite the dust I wondered? It felt pretty strong to me but disappointment was never far away in my world, so I had one eye on the engagement and the other on Shona. Just waiting for her to tell me this was all a huge mistake.
The getting engaged bit, so shortly after meeting really was a bad idea after all. I waited and waited for the disappointment but it never came. Then we were at Stansted airport, boarding the plane to Edinburgh on a morning flight. We arrived at the Templar Lodge Hotel and were treated like Royalty. We had free food, a fine double room and life sure seemed magical. Not a bookmakers in sight, so no chance of me slipping into the familiar routine and spoiling a great occasion. We spent the day familiarising ourselves with the surrounding unspoilt beauty, just readily preparing ourselves for the next day and the engagement in Roslyn chapel. Roslyn steeped in Knights Templar history and its renowned fame was certain to make the day all the more exciting. The day finally arrived and we set off to Roslyn, it was about twenty minutes from our hotel. We arrived to be greeted by monstrous scaffolding and it resembling a building site. Enfolding this quaint and beautiful church it was awful. We walked towards the door and opened it. Wow the energy of the place as before was awesome! You could even visualise the events of past as you walked in. No one was about, so I put the solitaire diamond ring I had bought Shona into a

single blood red rose, then went down on one knee and proposed. Luckily for me, although I felt a pratt, I never looked like one after as she accepted my offer! Job done now engaged. I felt excitement tinged with bewilderment at the speed of the whole process. Only time would tell if this fairytale beginning would indeed manifest into a lifetime commitment. Whatever the future may bring this visit went perfectly well and we were delighted. During this particular stay we decided that it would be a good idea to use the hotel for a conference on the paranormal and some months later we would return to fulfil this ambition. We arrived at Stansted airport and could hear wolf whistling and a mass of cheering. On looking up we saw a stag party and some bloke dressed as Madonna with a golden boob tube. I am bloody glad I won't be sitting next to that I thought. Time for our flight was pressing, so I popped to the toilet. On my return three Irishmen were talking to Shona. One said "would you like to come to Ireland with me?" "I don't think my boyfriend would be too happy." "I am not asking him!" was his witty reply. When I came back after a further three minutes they were still rabbiting away and my mood changed from happy to none best pleased and they moved on. What a flight that was. For a start the seats filled rapidly on the budget airline, and it began to look very ominous that Shona and myself would be seated in different parts of the plane. What was even worse was my realisation that I was going to be the slice of ham in a sandwich, of two people the size of whales. (I certainly have nothing against oversized people mind). But having to sit sideways for an hour or more was as appealing as Baghdad market during air strikes. Bloody hell! I had no choice one seat left that was it. I sat between these two people and I had to sit at an angle. It was dreadful. My stomach almost emptied its contents as the lady on my right pulled a rather large creamed doughnut out of her bag and stuffed it into her mouth sideways! No wonder you're bloody fat I thought. To make matters worse, her husband sitting on my left, pulled out a sandwich that was filled with some yellow substance, possibly mayonnaise and I had to watch as it dripped from the sides of the mouth. It couldn't get any worse could it? I desperately needed to move but didn't want to cause offence. I could feel my body heat rising, it was a nightmare. I managed God knows how to turn my head and spotted one more seat. I don't bloody believe it! I thought as I saw this blond wig, a golden boob tube top and some Pratt dressed as Madonna on his stag do surrounded by his friends. What could be worse than being squashed between two outsize people? Sitting next to Madonna with hairy legs and stubble and a stag do. 'Fu** it I thought! Just my bloody luck. Shona asked if I could sit there, to which they're testosterone levels exploded as they invited Shona to sit with them instead! By this time my blood was boiling. I leapt out of my particular fat people sandwich and plonked myself next to Madonna, (much to his annoyance no doubt). That was one hell of a flight and one I shall never forget. With Shona as a partner it had truly strengthened my resolve to get the truth out there. Shona herself is a very talented intuitive and it helps when I may miss something as she will pick it up. Mind you it has its drawbacks she bloody knows what you are up too! We had originally intended to marry at Roslyn on St George's day 2004 but the vicar there wouldn't have a medieval wedding in the church

and no way would he have me dressed as a Templar walking up the aisle. I thought the Templars were an integral part of Roslyn chapel. And after all it's what brings the coffers in. They don't go to see the Vicar there now do they? "You can't offend the Scots by having the flag of St George flying on that day" he said. What a twit! So after a few weeks trying to convince the inconvincible, we gave up on Roslyn as a wedding venue and chose another one namely Chillingham Castle instead. Chillingham is apparently one of Britain's most haunted castles. "Wow, that sounds great" said Shona. "Sounds perfect for a medieval Wedding" "I agree." "Right then, bags packed off to Chillingham." We were a little disappointed on our arrival at the place. More so when we got in there and I could see Shona wasn't as sold on the idea of marriage there now having seen the place in reality. We tried to spend the night in what supposedly is the most haunted room but had to settle for second best, another haunted room. Whilst sitting for a coffee in the tea room we talked about most haunted a television programme on living TV and happened to mention Yvette Fielding. "That is my husband's ex" said a voice from behind us. "We are staying in the Grey apartment tonight, why don't you join us later for a ghost vigil?" "Great idea, thanks see you after tea!" Her partner looked a bit shell shocked at her suggestion. We later found out he had planned a very romantic strawberries and cream picnic, champagne, night of passion job and his new wife's idea of us joining them was not conducive with his idea. The poor chap! Thankfully all went well.
We met them much later in the evening. We did have a couple of funny experiences there as sparks flew from the heater, we smelt some awful odour

and saw some orbs etc. I must admit that the place was eerie and a midnight walk past the dungeons is hardly conducive with good fun. Anyway we retired to our room fairly late and survived the night there. We didn't see any manifestations but we both felt that Chillingham certainly had a presence or two there. A ghost hunter's paradise wouldn't be far wrong and it was great fun. But no wedding there for us! Boy were we fed up with living in London, the area we lived in was a s***hole quite frankly.
I spoke to my guide John and asked if there was any chance of getting the hell out of there. I couldn't believe what I was getting, when he told me that we would be out of the flat come January. Bloody hell, are you sure? It's November now! The following day Shona got a message from her guides (inner voices) about a place called Heydon Hall. "Where's that?" I asked. "It is in Norfolk" she replied. "Just maybe they might do weddings?" she went on to say. "Well at least it wouldn't be as far as Chillingham for the family and guests to travel.
The following week we travelled up to Heydon hall, after the owner gave us some hope that he might be willing to let the venue for our wedding. He did however say that it is not something he does normally so we didn't get our hopes up too much. "Come and see me and we can discuss it." He added. On arriving in Heydon, I was amazed at how beautiful the area was. Shona told me it was a private village owned by a local family. As we entered the village we approached two white gates marked private on our left. We drove to the end of the drive and saw a workman. "Have you come about the cottage?" "That's interesting Shona did you hear what he said?" "No, in fact we have come about the hall for our wedding. We were told where

to find the owner and eventually we found the gentleman we needed. After some gentle persuasion he agreed to let us have our reception there. What about the Church in the village? Could we marry there? It's only two minutes from the reception? "I believe you would have to live in the village to do that" said the owner's son. "Ah, right. Someone has just mentioned a cottage you have here, is it available?" "Yes" he replied. Within five weeks we had left London and had set up home in Norfolk. Just as my spirit guides (inner voices) had predicted. Funnily enough one of their families from the past, Bulwer-Lytton wrote many novels. He is famous for his line 'the pen is mightier than the sword' quotation. He was also a leading Rosicrucian. We took a look at the local church which hopefully was to be our wedding venue and it was fabulous. Amazingly enough it has a Knights Templar ceremonial shield hung on the wall there. So it was in keeping with the rest of our story. We now had our hearts set on a St Georges day wedding in the beautiful village of Heydon and within days preparations had begun. I found out that Heydon has historical links to the Templars and the crusades. So everything appeared perfect. Destiny truly had come home. Only four months to go until the big day and a medieval wedding as predicted by my spirit friends. We now needed to organise costumes etc, mine and Shona's special outfits to make this all a reality. A rather strange event happened when we had a cup of tea in the local tea room there. I spotted a card with the name Sir Anthony Rawlinson written on it. It said he did photography. We needed a good photographer so I telephoned him when I got home. As I was talking to him I felt he was to be the best man (even though

that was the first time I had ever spoken to him and I/we had never met him). So I asked him and he agreed. He did our wedding portrait and was indeed our best man. How many people can say their best man when invited was someone they never even knew! Truth is sometimes stranger than fiction.
I remember Shona telling me she had a dream and had dreamt that everything was a last minute panic. 'I know that already' I thought. I never said anything to her for fear of making it worse. It was always going to be a panic! We took a trip to meet the Vicar and were pleased he had a good sense of humour, but would he still be laughing when we told him about our very different medieval wedding plan? Remembering the Roslyn chapel vicar (our first intended place of wedlock debacle) which was a nightmare! Still, all's well that ends well so they say and if Heydon's vicar was more understanding then we would indeed end up being happy bunnies. Hoorah! The Vicar was fine with the idea of a medieval wedding. In fact I think he was quite happy to see something different. What a nightmare I had getting my Templar outfit. Tunic, coif, hauberk, cape etc. some of the outfit came from Malta just 10 days before the wedding. An outfit beautifully hand made by Mr Charles Maignon. Talk about panic! Shona had more luck with the wedding dress in that the first dress she saw in a bridal magazine was the one she wanted (there is a God above)! I could envisage four months of hell trying to select a dress, but as the saying goes it was meant to be and it was. My inner voice had told me that the day would be a beautiful sunny day for the wedding one year in advance. In fact it p****d down with rain nearly all through April, all except a few days and our wedding day which was heaven

sent, it was 70 degrees! My inner voice also told me there would be film crews there on the big day. It turned out that both Anglia TV and the BBC sent film crews, newspapermen, radio interviews, the lot. It was unbelievable. We had Jousting knights, Jesters, fanfares, two gowned horses (Shona's horse's gown embroidered with gold swans) brought us to the church. Sir Anthony Rawlinson (best man) carrying a pole with the flag of St George flying high and proud, and my son Adam dressed as a Templar just like dad, led us in a procession. It was a truly magical day. Just think only a year and a half earlier I had never known or met Shona, then I saw her picture and knew it was all destined to be. It happened as predicted we would and did get engaged on Valentine's Day 2003 at Roslyn and we would and did get married on St Georges Day 2004 in a medieval wedding. I also knew the Sun would shine gloriously on that special day, the day of the joining of souls. The whole medieval wedding captured the hearts and minds of many on such a special day, our day, Shakespeare's & England's Day.

*`Thou hast no faults or I no faults can spy;*
*Thou art all beauty or all blindness I –*
*Christopher Coddrington 1668-1710*

## *THE PERFECT DAY*

*Gary & Shona's wedding day April 23rd 2004*

# Chapter Twelve

## *THE HONEYMOON*

After the magnificent wedding came the honeymoon. We decided a trip to California would make the perfect honeymoon. The flight was a bit bumpy but we were excited to be on our way.
We stayed at the Hyatt Hotel on Sunset Boulevard known as the riot house due to the rock stars that had previous stayed there. Fortunately that was in the past and we were pleasantly surprised by our surroundings. We were greeted on our arrival by a Steve Martin lookalike. "Goodness me, Shona. He looks more like Steve Martin than Steve Martin." If I was him I would have earnt a fortune as a top lookalike rather than a concierge. I became more convinced it was him when I stole a cheeky kiss from the mrs only for the lift to open just at that point with a smiling concierge saying "here's the honeymooners." This made us laugh!
After a couple of days of settling in we had a stroll down Sunset Boulevard where a black vagrant asked if I could spare any change. "Sorry, I don't have anything on me. I will bring you something on my way back I promise." True to my word on our return I handed the vagrant $10. He was overjoyed and told us he was a former Vietnam vet who was once bought a $1000 suit by Johnny Depp and had been given something by another famous celebrity Bet Midler. "I must do something for you" he said. "There is no need for that, just enjoy the money" I replied. "No. I insist" with that he burst into song singing a chorus from Elton John's hit 'Your song' and when it came to the bit 'how wonderful life is when you're in the world' he pointed at me and

Shona. It brought a tear to our eyes I can tell you. We invited him for breakfast at the famous Mel's 50's diner but he never came and we never saw him again. We wonder what became of him and how sad it was that his life was as it was. If any readers recognise this man from what I have said I would love to hear from them. It was it 2004 so a long time ago but it is worth asking. A man now surely forgotten by time but a memory we shall treasure for a lifetime.

We decided a trip to Vegas days later would make the perfect trip and headed off. On the way a thought popped into mind that we would stay at a ranch. We stopped at a diner for something to eat and fuel at Bairstow and noticed on the food menu that there was an advertisement for Calico Ghost Town. "Let's go there shall we?" said Shona. "Why not. Sounds fun!" I replied. We reached Calico which was just a short drive away. On entering the town we came across a few shops including a photo shop run by Bill and Jill. We had a photo done with old time western clothing on and asked Jill if there was anywhere local we could stay? There is nothing around here now she said. "That is a shame" I said. We began to talk about things in general and we mentioned to her about ghosts and our interest in things such. "I am very interested in that?" She said. "We have ghosts tours here run by myself and husband Bill. Why don't you come?" "We are off to Vegas soon but could come back I guess" I said. "You can stay with us we have a ranch nearby" "that would be fantastic". With that we headed off to Vegas and enjoyed a couple of days there coming back with shirt intact and not losing it on the roulette. On arriving back at Calico we went on to

Jill's ranch and stayed there for a week causing great amusement when I took her horse Stanley out for a ride. Fresh as a daisy he proceeded to do as he wanted and not what I told him. She introduced us to two friends of theirs Glen and Bill at the Ghost hunt we had arranged. Glen was a former forensics cop and Bill a bike rider for California US Governor Arnold Schwarzenegger. It was the most amazing evening as we saw people manifesting from thin air dressed in period clothing walking across the town only to disappear into thin air. I couldn't believe my eyes. Shona had a vision of a little girl and her description was of someone that Glen had seen before. Shona heard clanging of money at one spot and it turned out that was the origin of the assaying office. I was also pushed in the back but no one was there. It is a magical place I can tell you. The guys showed us some remarkable footage taken from previous hunts at Calico. One they called the walking man which was a ghostly figure and an incredible close up picture of a face moving backwards and forwards at the rock shop where they sold precious stones. It was truly astonishing footage. Sadly they have never published this material to my knowledge which is a great shame. We also had another remarkable experience with Glen and Bill on a visit to a place called the Pasadena playhouse. A large orb appeared and changed shape in front of our eyes; this was also recorded on camera. Some say an orb is just dust but this was one hell of a ball of dust. I am not easily convinced I like facts but I am certain of what I saw that day at Pasadena and at Calico. It certainly was a great privilege spending time with those guys and as a bonus Bill took us to see the place where the Governor sat in his office, not many will ever get the chance to see that. It was just another exciting adventure on our magical road.

After we left Calico we took in a visit to the Queen Mary in Long Beach. As we entered the ship we couldn't believe our ears as the song we had at our wedding 'Elizabethan Serenade' began to play on the ship. What are the odds on that happening? Our honeymoon to America had certainly been a magical trip.

We now conclude the book with one more remarkable and extraordinary event to discuss. Sheila who played an important part in my journey as told in the book was visiting a flat I had in London. I was there with John Roberts, a friend. I came out with a rather odd statement, when turning to John. "You know John you have lived many lives before and died many violent deaths but not in this life." I wasn't a believer in reincarnation although I was somewhat open minded to the concept. I then turned to Sheila and said "I can't say the same for you" Sheila was non plused by this "I am off to bed" she replied. And off she went. "I don't why John but I keep getting fire with Sheila. On the 14th June 2017 shortly after midnight, I lie in bed and put the radio on. The presenter said there had been an ongoing incident. A fire is raging in a block of flats in London. As more details were revealed they mentioned Latimer road and Holland Park. "Oh God, that isn't where Sheila lived?" I thought to myself. I had only visited Sheila once at her home. She had a beautiful flat on the 16th floor number132. I rushed downstairs to the computer and traced my footsteps back from the Starbucks café, we often sat at Holland Park putting the world to rights. I couldn't believe it as I saw that it was Sheila's block on fire.

I knew when I saw that my friend Sheila had perished in the Grenfell tower disaster. At school I was in Grenfell house, I had a connection to Latimer road and we both had a son named Adam. How remarkable is that? Now almost 20 years on or near as damn it since I had told John Roberts of Sheila's violent death and I kept getting fire that evening in London, one must wonder if it was pre-destined all along? Whatever the case may be I had seen into the future. A truly tragic end to her life, she was a most beautiful soul. Life and death is such a mystery and my experiences along the road have made those mysteries even more difficult to comprehend. Life goes on and we all continue to learn and go through differing experiences of joy, love, hurt, loss and pain. Perhaps one day you too will seek and find the magical path on your journey in search of the swan and the third great step of spiritual enlightenment.

*`You can call spirits from the vasty deep why,*
*So can I, or so can any man, but will*
*they come when you do call them?'*
*William Shakespeare*

*Footnote*:

After appearances on TV and radio I realised getting the truth out would not be easy. It is not my intention to prove or disprove my gifts. The mind as we know it is a powerful thing but what is absolutely undeniable is that not all I have produced can possibly be from my own vivid imagination. Believing that would be simply folly. The stories contained within this book are factual and nothing has been added or taken away to dramatise the events in any way. All I can tell others is my story. If people want to believe or disbelieve then either way that is fine by me. My aim is to provoke thought and if it does that then this book has served its purpose. The reason I put the information relating to Shakespeare in the book is it is such an important part of my journey, and without it the book would not be the same. I understand for some Shakespeare and facts about his life and others connected to him may appear as irrelevant, but I feel it most important in the wider scheme of enlightenment. Is the book controversial? Perhaps, but all I infer is this, it is my truth as in factual and what I found to be right. For others they too must search for theirs. I have mentioned the great white brotherhood in my book which links to the theosophists and Madame Blavasky. I am not a fan of Blavatsky and the channelling she did. I find many aspects of it dubious. However the link to the swan has great significance, so it was important to mention it. My life experiences and story has simply been remarkable. What if I had never met Maggie on the train all those years ago? What if I had never given her that message before she exited at the very next stop? Would I have ever been in

Norfolk? Would I have ever met Shona? How would my life have been now? I know its all 'what if' but sometimes we need to act in the moment, I did. We may not always understand but sometimes we don't have to. If we go with our heart and our mind wondrous things can happen, they did to me and they could to you! I had become a master of conversing with spirits and understood after almost 30 years of communication they in part can be the great deceivers so the need for great care is advised, but what couldn't be doubted was their existence. My material proved that. It is also worth mentioning a flaw has never been found in my abilities. I believe and am certain that we all have the (for want of a better word) 'gifts' of healing and the sixth sense, intuition, psychic ability (all names for the same thing, call them what you like). They are natural abilities within us all, we just need to find and understand them. I also believe that I prove the mind survives death through my work and writings.

Finally I dedicate the book 'In Search of the Swan' to all those who became part of the journey to enlightenment in whatever way, large or small and especially to my beautiful wife Shona, who has travelled this road with me so selflessly and endured the highs and lows of 'the Cockney Bard,' a name given to me by Shona, unbeknown to her at the time but as we later found out was in fact a derogatory term given to John Keats in the early 18oo's. I say a massive heartfelt thank you. I also dedicate this book to all those freethinkers who have passed, are present now and will in the future come.

Gary Allen (the Cockney Bard)

Printed in Dunstable, United Kingdom

65727372R00109